I Am

I Am

A STUDY OF E. E. CUMMINGS' POEMS

Gary Lane

THE UNIVERSITY PRESS OF KANSAS
Lawrence/Manhattan/Wichita

© Copyright 1976 by The University Press of Kansas
Manufactured in the United States of America
Designed by Fritz Reiber

Library of Congress Cataloging in Publication Data

Lane, Gary, 1943-
I am: a study of E. E. Cummings' poems.

Bibliography: p.
Includes index.
1. Cummings, Edward Estlin, 1894-1962—Criticism
and interpretation. I. Title.
PS3505.U334Z73   811'.5'2   75-38757
ISBN 0-7006-0142-2
ISBN 0-7006-0144-9 pbk.

Grateful acknowledgment is made for permission to quote from the following poets:

JOHN BERRYMAN. From *The Dream Songs*. Copyright 1969 by John Berryman. Reprinted by permission of Farrar, Straus & Giroux, Inc.

HART CRANE. From *The Complete Poems and Selected Letters and Prose of Hart Crane*, edited with an Introduction and Notes by Brom Weber. Copyright 1933, © 1958, 1966, by Liveright Publishing Corporation. Used with permission.

E. E. CUMMINGS. The poetry of E. E. Cummings is reprinted from his volume *Complete Poems 1913–1962* by permission of Harcourt Brace Jovanovich, Inc.; copyright 1923, 1925, 1931, 1935, 1940, 1944, 1948, 1949, 1951, 1958, 1959 by E. E. Cummings; copyright 1963, 1968 by Marion Morehouse Cummings; copyright 1972 by Nancy T. Andrews.

DANTE. From *Dante's Divine Comedy*, translated by Louis Biancolli. Copyright 1966 by Louis Biancolli. Reprinted by permission of Washington Square Press.

JAMES DICKEY. From *Poems 1957–1967*. Copyright © 1964 by James Dickey. Reprinted by permission of Wesleyan University Press.

EMILY DICKINSON. From *The Complete Poems of Emily Dickinson*, edited by Thomas H. Johnson. Copyright 1929, © 1957 by Mary L. Hampson. Reprinted by permission of Little, Brown and Company.

T. S. ELIOT. From *Collected Poems 1909–1963*. Copyright by T. S. Eliot. Reprinted by permission of Harcourt Brace Jovanovich, Inc.

ROBERT FROST. From *Selected Poems of Robert Frost*. Copyright 1963 by Robert Frost.

This book
is dedicated to the memory
of

Edward Lane

because my father lived his soul
love is the whole and more than all

ACKNOWLEDGMENTS

Like most studies, this book is the sum of more indebtedness than can be adequately acknowledged. Cummings' critics, particularly Norman Friedman and Barry Marks, broke ground in their books for whatever insights I erect here; their sensitivity to the poet helped teach me how and where to read him. Friends and colleagues, too, at both the University of Michigan and the University of Miami, proved invaluable. Gary Stein, Isabel Reade, and Bonnie Greenberg made helpful suggestions about individual poems; Peter Bauland tried, not always successfully, to commend the virtues of a plain style; and Thomas Garbaty offered encouragement at a crucial time. Lyall Powers read, criticized, and supported the work at every stage, and Clark Emery, who read the penultimate draft, forced me to reconsider my position on several poems. Least definable but by no means least important is my debt to Carmen Brummet, whose faith never precluded her insistence on clarity.

At the start of my work, Harcourt Brace Jovanovich inspirited me by releasing a full American edition of the text; *Complete Poems 1913–1962* includes even "the boys i mean are not refined," a holographic poem previously limited to a few signed copies of *No Thanks*. With Harcourt's kind permission, it is from this volume, lovingly prepared by the poet's bibliographer, George J. Firmage, that I quote. In the beginning, too, I was aided by a grant from the Lutheran Church in America's Board of College Education. In somewhat different form, the discussions of two poems, "sonnet entitled how to run the world)" and "yes is a pleasant country:," appeared previously in the pages of the *Explicator*. They are used here through that journal's courtesy.

CONTENTS

his royal warcry is I AM
and he's the soul of chivalry

—CP 774

ABBREVIATIONS

References to the poems and letters of E. E. Cummings are identified within the body of the text according to the following scheme of abbreviation:

> *CP* is *E. E. Cummings: Complete Poems 1913–1962* (New York: Harcourt Brace Jovanovich, 1972).
>
> *L* is *Selected Letters of E. E. Cummings*, ed. F. W. Dupee and George Stade (New York: Harcourt, Brace & World, 1969).

1

INTRODUCTION

In all my lectures, I have taught one doctrine, namely, the infinitude of the private man.

—Ralph Waldo Emerson,
Journals

I

Whose poems are E. E. Cummings'? Antitheses beckon
in reply. Are they the poems of an arch classicist, radically
concerned with formal balance and traditional decorums, or
those of a radical modern, archly delighted with scattered
typography, omitted punctuation, and bawdy puns? Are they
songs of the lyrical sonneteer, chivalrously singing his love and
his lady, or blasts of the indignant satirist, savagely caricatur-
ing the fools he saw everywhere? Are they poems of an eternal
romantic, lover of nature, selfhood, and organic wholeness, or
those of a contemporary realist, knower of fear and fragmen-
tation? Replying to another dichotomous question, Cummings
answered as he would have for the alternatives just offered:
"And why not both?"[1] The poet—certainly this poet—is many
selves.

Labels group and limit, and so deceive; applying them to
a poet fundamentally concerned with the uniqueness of the
individual can scarcely help us to discover his poems. Besides,
Cummings knew Emerson's famous dictum on hobgoblins—
the Concord essayist later rephrased it "Damn Consistency!"
—and for him too "the infinitude of the private man" sub-
sumed all system.[2] We will best approach these poems, then,
without pigeonholes, expecting anything. Much will not be
there, of course—Marianne Moore observes that "it is useless to
search [Cummings' work] for explanations, reasons, becauses,"[3]
and probably among major poets of our time Cummings is the
narrowest in choice of subject—but emotional and aesthetic
integrity is constant. Because of it, these words of a dead man
can move us to earned intensities of feeling, can modify the
guts of the living.

II

Modification is what Cummings sought. He is among the
company of poets who tell us always, either explicitly or by

implication, how to live; though of course for these as for any poets, the way of saying is an essential part of the thing said. Further, Cummings sought modification through intensity—he tried to board his readers at a station deeper than intellect—and thus, whether we deal with the tricky but overt instructions of the "sonnet entitled how to run the world)" (*CP* 390) or the unspecified commitments that underlie "All in green went my love riding" (*CP* 14), we must pay particular attention in his poetry to the unity of idea and expression. Though it will sometimes be expedient to talk of these as if each had independent existence, this *caveat* must right that notion. Cummings' intensity lives almost entirely in the marriage of spirited conception and linguistic flesh; divorce these or make one subservient, and what vanishes is poetry.

That said, it will be well to sketch in this introductory chapter Cummings' visions and revisions, his ways of seeing the universe and his ways of making poems from what he saw. Though later chapters are organized to help demonstrate the coherence of Cummings' thought and work—each follows a motif as it expands into a major theme, and each grows toward a larger sense of the whole by assimilating the preceding chapters' technical and thematic discoveries—the focus of those later chapters is narrowed to specific poems, where, after all, the magic is. Here at the start we may seek an overview, a look at the forest whose trees are to be examined.

Such perspective will be particularly useful in reading Cummings, for the outline of his work has been sometimes mistaken by those who fail to relate the parts to the whole. Losing the forest for the trees, these readers suppose it either an impenetrable jungle—"[Cummings'] work is inchoate, perverse, vicious when not merely meaningless"[4]—or a trivial grove: "In his serious moods, he writes sentimentally about love, conceived primarily as copulation; in his satirical moments, he makes smutty jokes about it."[5] A broad glance at the poet's thematic concerns will help us avoid such nearsighted surveying. It will facilitate the integration of specific poems into a general vision and prepare us for later conclusions: that nothing in Cummings' work, whether failed or fully achieved, is perverse or vicious or careless; and that the poet's contextual treatment of love, copulation, and sexual humor, assessing spiritual rather than surface meaning, reflects a judgment both coherent and wholesome.

III

The more than seven hundred pieces comprising *Complete Poems 1913–1962* make up a single vast *Song of Myself*. Behind every poem—chivalrous love lyric, satirical tirade, moral fable, or impressionist word-painting—we have an exceptionally strong sense of the poet's presence, for Cummings, relentlessly subjective, insists always upon the sanctity of his personal, private vision; each poem, whatever else it sings, sings also "I am," its maker's dynamic existence. This is at once a weakness and a strength. Because egocentricity did not lead Cummings to Whitman's all encompassing tolerance, there is about his poetry a surface of arrogance. "What I like least about Cummings' poems," wrote Randall Jarrell, "is their pride in Cummings and their contempt for most other people. . . . All his work thanks God that he is not as other men are; none of it says, 'Lord, be merciful to me, a sinner.'"[6] But Cummings combined his authentic prelapsarianism with an evangelical fervor, he added a moral imperative to his cheerful certainty that men and their dreams, far from fallen, fall only when they refuse to rise. Quick with a Nietzschean contempt—why coddle a slave who could be master?—he is also quick with reverence; his disdain is the world-knowing response of an unceasing idealism. The intransigence of that idealism may distance the poet from many who reject it, but to the absolutist, tolerance lacks integrity. Cummings felt his values strongly, and felt that only in maintaining them could he proceed as a man and a poet. "The proper study of Mankind is Man," Pope had learned from Aristotle, and for Cummings the obvious man to start with was himself. He staked out the local but limitless territory of his own heart, and for fifty years he worked that claim ever deeper.

Egocentricity did not isolate Cummings, however; in truth, it hardly distinguished him from anyone else. In his Harvard nonlectures, the poet slyly noted that "half a century of time and several continents of space, in addition to a healthily developed curiosity, haven't yet enabled me to locate a single peripherally situated ego."[7] What did distinguish Cummings' stance was the forthrightness with which he embraced his egotism. We find in his work little of the moral acedia or compulsive self-laceration that characterize so much modern poetry, but rather an unquestioning conviction—almost the mystic's intuited faith—in his own, and in man's, natural divinity. Cummings saw, of course, that men were often stupid, cruel, and self-destructive, but he rejected the dehumanizing comfort of sociological and psychological determinism, and never shunted responsibility for the world's failure away from individuals. Instead, he stood resolutely by his dialectic of love, death, and growth, the strenuous cycle through which a man might transcend his own and the world's limitations.[8]

That dialectic, unspoken as doctrine but inescapable in the poems, is crucial to understanding Cummings, for implicit in its operation are the forces that unify his apparently antipodal selves. The dialectic links the ethereal ideal with an earthy reality—"my father gave me Plato's metaphor of the cave with my mother's milk,"[9] Cummings wrote, symbolizing, perhaps unconsciously, the twin poles that compassed his thought—and it suggests at the same time the formidable self-discipline needed for their connection. Love, whether of man or truth, is a terrible beauty, a naked giving of self; "It is to be learned—/ . . . But only by the one who/ Spends out himself again."[10] Once learned, though, love leads through metaphoric or physical death to spiritual growth; and whether the attendant losses are of social acceptance, as with "anyone" and "noone" (*CP*

515), or earthly life, as with Olaf (*CP* 339), the dynamic transcendence of lovers outweighs in a new world what they gave up in an old.

Cummings, then, is hardly the single-minded libertine that disingenuous moralists sometimes make him. Far from conceiving of love "primarily as copulation," he imagined it to be part of any free-spirited giving. When this giving was present in sexuality, Cummings honored it as gladly as when it appeared elsewhere, but when the love-making turned to something less, Cummings turned to satire. His contempt for the mechanical prostitute of "raise the shade" (*CP* 109) is as characteristic as his sympathy for the casual but generous lovers of "may i feel said he" (*CP* 399); both are based on the poet's eye not for social situation or external appearance but for spiritual reality. If Cummings praises a different whore in another poem, it is in Nietzsche's spirit, for, like Nietzsche, Cummings moved beyond good and evil; his judgments took root not in deprivation, the conventional morality of "Thou shalt not," but in affirmation, and he affirmed the beauty of love whatever its form.

IV

Cummings affirmed, too, the love of form as a root of beauty. Behind the celebrated but superficial controversies over his capitalization, punctuation, and spacing, there stands the abundant evidence of the poems, and these show clearly a poet's concern with form. Cummings put it simply: "If a poet is anybody, he is somebody . . . obsessed by Making" (*CP* 223). His own obsession with making led him to highly organized, highly formal work, poems whose wholeness has much to do with the congruence of images, the coherence of sounds, the balance of lines. As a boy he had passed beyond the idea that what "mattered about any poem . . . was what the poem said; its socalled meaning";[11] instead, seeking "that precision which creates movement" (*CP* 223), he turned "from substance to structure."[12]

This last phrase is not to be misunderstood. Cummings always retained a firm commitment to the "substance" of his personal truth—he never ceased telling his readers how to live —but he discovered quite early that poetry works prior to intellection, that it communicates feelings rather than ideas, and that only through the imaginative organization of the poet— the inspiration and hard work that underlie structural coherence—can a poet generate significant intensity. Such an aesthetic echoed his broader vision, for form involves both the eternal and the immediate, a transcending of flux and an embrace of it, "Plato's metaphor of the cave" and "my mother's milk." A form "can and does exist in and of itself"[13]—"whatever a ballade may be about, it is always a ballade"[14]—but it takes life from the heft and edge of its experiential matter.

We can extend this distinction to the general category of poetic technique. A poet's task is to convey through verbal structure the emotional substance of experience, for only if he does so can the natural vitality of that experience survive its transplant to the valley of poetic making. Cummings pursues this task in a manner reminiscent of the metaphysical poets: he tries to surprise us into vision, all the while marshalling his surprises in a formal pattern that makes them seem, if not inevitable, then certainly just. Pun, paradox, inversion of cliché, grammatical turning—these are but a few of the means by which this most inventive poet commands our attention; and at his best Cummings is equally noteworthy for the discipline with which he applies them. In the following short poem, for example, vulgarity paradoxically illustrates the decorum of effect in Cummings' work:

> red-rag and pink-flag
> blackshirt and brown
> strut-mince and stink-brag
> have all come to town

some like it shot
and some like it hung
and some like it in the twot
nine months young   (*CP* 497)

No commentary on "socalled meaning" is needed here. One recognizes the *Walpurgisnacht* assemblage of Communists, Fascists, and Nazis in the first two lines, and the murder and rape that follow are only too historically accurate. What matters in this poem is the emotion that Cummings' surprises—the disparity between innocent nursery rhyme and corrupt experience, the vulgar slang of the penultimate line—move us toward. In the assimilation of Mother Goose's rhythm by goose-stepping storm troops, and in the application to the love act of the seventh line's merciless meter and harsh final stop, Cummings forces us to feel the "ceremony of innocence . . . drowned."[15]

This striving for immediacy of effect, the constant point of Cummings' technique, explains the poet's much debated penchant for verbal and typographical experiment. In one poem, he paints simply a full "mOOn Over tOwns" (*CP* 383), the capital "O"s engaging our sense of visual as well as linguistic representation. In another, he makes graphic a comparison, evoking the break and fall of ocean waves by spacing and decorative punctuation: clouds must indeed be evanescent if they are more

```
                    forge
      tful:e
           ver than,is e
                ven:th
                    e(s
                      e
                    a's;m
                      e,
                       m(or.y   (CP 447)
```

In a third, Cummings creates a kind of complex ideogram, using unusual line breaks to give his poem at once a feeling of

the action named and a visual picture of that action's symbolic
sum:

<pre>
   l(a

   le

   af

   fa

   ll

   s)

   one

   l

   iness   (CP 673)
</pre>

Sensing here, like Hopkins' Margaret, the human condition in
a falling leaf, Cummings images its descent in the short, verti-
cal shape of his poem. At the same time, and in the same shape,
he draws the number 1. This startling double existence generates the poem's emotion by identifying its root: we are lonely
because we are one, and it is our essential individuality that
links us with each dying leaf. When we note that the typewritten letter "l" is identical to the typewritten number "1,"
we can watch the poem's equation—l = i = lonely—turn over
and over with its descending leaf. From the "l" of the first
line, the ideogram gathers feeling until its climactic triple repetition: "one/ 1// iness." Such skillful typographic shorthand
enables Cummings to give language the impact of first speech.

   A similar intent underlies the poet's more purely linguistic
devices. In "anyone lived in a pretty how town" (CP 515), the
prickly-pear-rounding townsfolk are neatly introduced in a
distorted cliché that tells all. "Women and men(both little
and small" are the dull multitudes, too somnolent even for
quiet desperation; Cummings' alteration of "big and small,"
the usual phrase and usual mixture, conveys no mere homoge-
neity but a mortifying shrinkage, emotional rather than fleshly.
A more complicated verbal effect is this description of two
homosexual British poets:

(neck and senecktie
are gentlemen ppoyds
even whose recktie
are covered by lloyd's   (CP 492)

Here pun, literary allusion, spelling that both imitates pronun-
ciation and creates sight rhyme, and erroneous Latin generate
wonderful satire. The twosome are "neck and [hi]s necktie,"
by implication inseparable, stiffly formal, and complementary
in a way that suggests sexual posture as well as style of dress;
their linguistic affectation is echoed in "ppoyds" for "poets,"
and their pseudo-intellectualism in "recktie" for "recta" (our
own word is rectums). That they must pose about even this
last, the need for particular anatomical coverage from London's
largest insurer, lends merriment to the devastation. Yet there
is a further, more serious point to all this. The first line quoted,
"(neck and senecktie," alludes to a famous ode of Horace,
wherein is lamented the inevitable drawing on of death:

> Eheu fugaces, Postume, Postume,
> labuntur anni, *nec* pietas moram
>   rugis et instanti *senectae*
>   afferet indomitaeque morti;
>   (II, xiv, 1–4; my italics)

> Alas, Postumus, Postumus, the flying
> years glide by, nor shall piety delay
>   wrinkles and stalking old age
>   and unconquerable death.

Echoing but turning this meditation, Cummings undermines
the *false* pieties of his two poets, the leftist platitudes they
mouth and the unnatural sexuality they practice: "vive the
millenni/ um three cheers for labor/ give all things to enni/
one bugger thy nabor" (CP 492). He reminds us that each of
these visitors, like the moribund everyman of the *Ode* quoted,
has left his lands, his house, and perhaps even a loved wife,
"tellus, et domus, et placens/ uxor" (II, xiv, 21–2); he implies

that the deliberate actions of these poets' lives mirror the estate of death in Horace.

A final example demonstrates one of the poet's characteristic verbal devices, altering the grammatical function of words:

> when god decided to invent
> everything he took one
> breath bigger than a circustent
> and everything began

> when man determined to destroy
> himself he picked the was
> of shall and finding only why
> smashed it into because (*CP* 566)

This little record of making and shattering, a testament to the creative power of imagination and abstracting's destructive force, uses Cummings' functional dislocations to significant effect. Within the framework of the whole poem, they establish the contrast between god's solitary and imagistic act—"he took one/ breath bigger than a circustent"—and man's collective and abstracted one: "he picked the was/ of shall and finding only why/ smashed it into because." Within the context of their stanza, these dislocations form an effective if scarcely paraphrasable metaphor. Man's self-destruction, we are told, is accomplished by needing to explain rather than wanting to experience; finding only "why," questions, when he attempts to set his collective destiny, man angrily smashes them, atoms at Hiroshima, into "because," the answers that he craves.

V

If this linguistically and technically experimental poet tried always to make us see anew, he could not have expected always to succeed. No writer bats a thousand. Despite Miss Moore's charitable assertion that "he does not make aesthetic mistakes,"[16] Cummings too has his share of failures. I think them worth dwelling upon for a moment, not to tarnish the fully achieved poems—what poet's work would not then be tarnished?—but to demonstrate the peculiar risks to which Cummings' experimentation made him liable.

Cummings' weak poems seem to me primarily of three kinds. There are songs of innocence whose childlike notes flatten into sentimentality, songs of experience, especially satires, whose thematic ideas are lost in linguistic experiment, and typographic vignettes whose ingenuity does not sustain poetic life. Of the first type, little need be said. In the pursuit of natural piety, the romantic, the transcendent poet occasionally forgets that although "The Child is father of the Man," he is himself "now . . . a man" and no longer a child.[17] We have Wordsworth's "Anecdote for Fathers" as immortal evidence of this error, and Cummings, whose search for the childlike sometimes led him into the very mouth of the child, also fell prey. An example is "little tree":

> who found you in the green forest
> and were you very sorry to come away?
> see   i will comfort you
> because you smell so sweetly
>
> i will kiss your cool bark
> and hug you safe and tight
> just as your mother would,
> only don't be afraid   (*CP* 192)

Though the poem continues for another sixteen lines, I find nothing distinctive in its child-speaker's response to the Christmas tree, nothing to rescue these feelings from sentimentality.[18]

Of the typographic vignettes, everything is response. Yet response, while it can partake of typographic surprises, must proceed from some alliance between the surprises and the language that forms them. Sometimes, prepossessedly experimenting with the unorthodox arrangement of words, Cummings pays insufficient attention to the words themselves. His famous grasshopper poem, an extreme example, is for this reason merely clever; because its words lack inner form, a manifestation of substance through surface, layout cannot give them life:

r-p-o-p-h-e-s-s-a-g-r
                    who
a)s w(e loo)k
upnowgath
          PPEGORHRASS
                    eringint(o-. . . (*CP* 396)

The plot here is pretty clear; the poem tells of an anagrammatic
grasshopper who, as we look up, now gathering into a The,
leaps, arriving to rearrangingly become—grasshopper. But
Cummings' spatial and typographical arrangements, though
they communicate that motion, do not succeed in making it
interesting; that necessary combination of precision and revela-
tion, achieved in the falling-leaf poem, is not managed in
"r-p-o-p-h-e-s-s-a-g-r."

Most damaging to Cummings have been satiric poems
whose linguistic experimentation leads them, and often their
readers, astray. An infamous example is this:

> a kike is the most dangerous
> machine as yet invented
> by even yankee ingenu
> ity(out of a jew a few
> dead dollars and some twisted laws)
> it comes both prigged and canted   (*CP* 644)

Though this controversial poem has been much discussed, it is
well to reiterate the chief point. The problem here is "kike,"
and it is a problem of usage rather than prejudice. Cummings
attempts to delineate and satirize not Jewishness but a particular class of Jews, the noisy, money-worshiping, self-satisfied,
advantage-taking few. His own comment is apropos:

> Whereas in unpopular parlance "a kike" equals a
> jew, for me "a kike" equals an UNjew. Why? Because
> for me a jew is a human being; whereas "a kike" is a
> machine—the product of that miscalled Americaniza-
> tion,alias standardization(id est dehumanization)
> which,from my viewpoint,makes out&out murder a rel-
> atively respectable undertaking.[19]

Granting the poem a spiritual legitimacy, however, does not make it a success. Cummings never surmounts here the connotative impediments of his first phrase; he has not properly felt the pulse of his language, sensed the twentieth-century vinegar and gall in "kike." Thus, despite the witty sexual puns of its final line, his poem never gathers effective satiric force. Its energy is not contained and directed, but dissipates in our concern over the explosive "kike"; and by the time we have defused that troublesome word, the poem, too, is quiet.

VI

Failure, of course, is the wages of risk; but in Cummings such wages are meager in comparison with the happier alternative. If I have spoken of several failed poems, it is in part to show that Cummings nods too, that later emphasis on the poet's significant achievements does not preclude an understanding of his limitations. Certainly, the later emphasis is strongly positive. I have selected for discussion work that lives, and chosen for each of my thematically arranged chapters five varied as well as excellent poems. Though such a scheme necessarily considers only a small fraction of Cummings' considerable canon, that evil seemed mitigable; full explicative treatments are the best way to demonstrate Cummings' imaginative and technical precision. Moreover, I have tried to exemplify a romantic principle—to reveal the general by focusing upon the particular—and I hope that this tour of points of major interest will facilitate further travel throughout the world of E. E. Cummings.

Ultimately, the experience of a poem is mysterious; at some point far subtler than any scholar can delineate, spoken or printed words intersect a receiving sensibility, and a birth occurs. My goal for this study is to help precipitate that birth. As my central chapters follow the course of Cummings' dialectic—they move from two aspects of love (seduction and selfhood) through two kinds of death (a true and a false) to the final unity of transcendent growth—they force a reader constantly back to the poems. There he should begin and end, for criticism, though it may order, clarify, and admire, can never take the place of that birth we call poetry.

2

A PLEASANT COUNTRY

1. Man has no Body distinct from his Soul; for that call'd Body is a portion of Soul discern'd by the five Senses, the chief inlets of Soul in this age.

2. Energy is the only life, and is from the Body; and Reason is the bound or outward circumference of Energy.

3. Energy is Eternal Delight.

—William Blake,
The Marriage of Heaven and Hell

"notice the convulsed orange inch of moon" (CP 86)

notice the convulsed orange inch of moon
perching on this silver minute of evening.

We'll choose the way to the forest—no offense
to you, white town whose spires softly dare.
Will take the houseless wisping rune
of road lazily carved on sharpening air.

Fields lying miraculous in violent silence

fill with microscopic whithering
. . .(that's the Black People, chérie,
who live under stones.) Don't be afraid

and we will pass the simple ugliness
of exact tombs, where a large road crosses
and all the people are minutely dead.

Then you will slowly kiss me

Seduction, traditionally the springtime pursuit of shy maids by sly logicians, is in Cummings' world a year-round, far more democratic enterprise. Now loftily formal, now ingeniously metaphoric, a variety of amorous young men caper through these poems, cajoling, beckoning, propositioning outright. Not merely common, however, theirs is a wholly honorable business, for to Cummings seduction involves a drawing together rather than a leading away; love is a lively surrender, a death that can lead to growth, and the poet welcomes it under any auspices.[1] To his development of this position, Cummings has brought a prodigious technical imagination and an uncompromising originality. Accepting the inheritance of tradition, he has not let it confine him, but sought continually to extend the resources of the past. And he has succeeded often enough to take his place in our century among the few masters of a small lyrical genre, the cavalier poem.

A striking sonnet, "notice the convulsed orange inch of moon" offers evidence of this mastery. Like every successful seduction poem, it is a triumph of strategy; unlike most, however, it is the triumph of a strategy particularly suited to its end. The poem's male speaker visualizes an activity we might call octobering—in essence, it is a-maying under the Halloween orange of a harvest moonsliver—and wishes to move his lady toward a similar desire. Avoiding the traditional lover's logic as perhaps inappropriate to the occasion—he wants, after all, to engage his lady's emotional being rather than her mind—he casts instead a spell, creates a magically heightened expectancy that ought to affect even the timidest fall Corinna.

Several elements conjoin toward the creation of this spell, notably tone, image, and language. From the start, the speaker's tone is self-assured, controlled; "notice," he begins, the imperative commanding attention as of a hypnotist's subject, and throughout the poem a prophetic future tense sustains this hypnotic confidence: "We'll choose the way to the forest," "Will take the houseless wisping rune/ of road," "and we will pass the simple ugliness/ of exact tombs." There is, then, a force of personality as well as of grammar when the lover concludes, "Then you will slowly kiss me." Lending effect, too, is the weight of image. The disappearing moon "perching on this silver minute of evening," the thinning autumn air, the "microscopic whithering" (a pun that links the elegist's *ubi sunt* with the simple decay of leaves), the ugly tombs—all serve to intensify the anticipatory presence of the occasion. No need, here, to point gracefully at the haste of Time's wingéd chariot; the immediate setting conveys it with emotional impact. Finally, the very resonance of language furthers the expectancy of the moment. The evening is magical—"rune" and "miraculous" imply what is made concrete by "the Black people . . ./ who live under stones"—and a ubiquitous activity seems the essence of all—"convulsed" moon, daring spires, "sharpening" air, "violent" silence, and "whithering" fields—save the "minutely dead."

There is a fine quality of wonder, innocent and transcendental, to this excitement. The spellbinding young lover is himself captivated by the natural miracles of love, autumn, and evening, and through the imaginative accuracy that Cummings grants him, he moves us to similar feelings. By the small linguistic violences of oxymoron and pun, we are shaken to fresh vision: "Fields lying miraculous in violent silence/ fill with microscopic whithering." The tentative, mysterious, precise deshabille of a forest road in fall becomes instantly, unalterably ours as we take with the lovers "the houseless wisping rune/ of road lazily carved on sharpening air." Ultimately, we are led by "that precision which creates movement" (*CP* 223) to identify with the poem's lovers. Celebrating motion in the face of entropy, they cheerfully transcend the melancholic background of Marvell. Against and over the "merely undeniable fact" of death, they set and rejoice in the "purely irresistible truth" (*CP* 223) of love.

"if i have made,my lady,intricate" (CP 306)

if i have made,my lady,intricate
imperfect various things chiefly which wrong
your eyes(frailer than most deep dreams are frail)
songs less firm than your body's whitest song
upon my mind—if i have failed to snare
the glance too shy—if through my singing slips
the very skilful strangeness of your smile
the keen primeval silence of your hair

—let the world say "his most wise music stole
nothing from death"—
                                you only will create
(who are so perfectly alive)my shame:
lady through whose profound and fragile lips
the sweet small clumsy feet of April came

into the ragged meadow of my soul.

"Beauty is momentary in the mind—" wrote Wallace Stevens, "The fitful tracing of a portal;/ But in the flesh it is immortal."[2] Fra Pandolf had spoken similarly of the Duchess: "Paint/ Must never hope to reproduce the faint/ Half-flush that dies along her throat."[3] Many artists, then, have understood that ideas of things—and aesthetic images of them, in music, paint, or words—are not the things themselves. This is the point that Cummings, classical sonneteer but with a twist, re-iterates in "if i have made,my lady,intricate." The early "Puella Mea" had seen him turning chivalric verses in a traditional groove (note even the echo of Yeats's "The Folly of Being Comforted"):

> If she a little turn her head
> i know that i am wholly dead:
> nor ever did on such a throat
> the lips of Tristram slowly dote,
> La beale Isoud whose leman was.[4]   (*CP* 17)

Here, however, Cummings finds a novelty that transforms vocal exercise to poem. Singing the graces of his lady, the poet confers no immortality; rather, paying her a greater compli-ment, he *fails* to immortalize her. Samuel Daniel's sonnets to Delia might be "the arks, the trophies I erect/ That fortify thy name against old age,"[5] but Cummings' "most wise music [steals]/ nothing from death." His lady's delicacy and nuance are such, her liveliness so subtle, as to defeat even the poet's powers of evocation. Thus, with a single stroke, Cummings goes the sonneteer's hyperbole one better, yet speaks words for which we need make no allowance.

The conceit is not entirely original, of course; six hundred years earlier, Petrarch had despaired of giving tongue to Laura's beauty.[6] But this poem, not only a reversal of one of the sonnet's classical themes, reverses as well one of its classic metaphors. In traditional fashion, the octave deals with the creativity of the poet-speaker. In the sestet, though, Cummings shows us something new: by a fine syntactic suspension—"you only will create/ (who are so perfectly alive)my shame"—he leads us to see not himself but his lady as the successful artist.

At the focal point of this structurally Italian sonnet, "i have made," the initial emphasis, shifts to the heightened chivalry of "you only will create."

Yet this is extravagant. The poet, too, creates; conditional "if," appearing three times, predicates the argument. Thus while on the one hand the speaker's uncertainty about art in the face of life is a graceful convention, a chivalrous metaphor for his lady's pleasing particularity, on the other it is a proposition to be tested by the poem itself. We are presented, as so often in Cummings' poems, with a paradox. Like Dylan Thomas, who in "A Refusal to Mourn the Death, by Fire, of a Child in London," "says what he says he will not say,"[7] Cummings contrives here to make what he makes out he cannot make, a poem that will evoke his lady's sublety, delicacy, and liveliness.

Not, let us note—and again this departs from tradition—her loveliness. Sidney had read "in Stella's face . . ./ What love and beauty be," found in her eyes "Nature['s] . . . chief work."[8] Petrarch, before him, had written of Laura,

> La testa or fino e calda neve il volto,
> ebeno i cigli e gli occhi eran due stelle,
> onde Amor l'arco non tendeva in fallo;
>
> perle e rose vermiglie, ove l'accolto
> dolor formava ardenti voci e belle;
> fiamma i sospir, le lagrime cristallo.

Her locks were gold, her cheeks were breathing snow,
Her brows with ebon arched—bright stars her eyes,
Wherein Love nestled, thence his dart to aim:

Her teeth were pearls—the rose's softest glow
Dwelt on that mouth, whence woke to speech grief's sighs;
Her tears were crystal—and her breath was flame.[9]

And Cummings himself had emphasized his lady's superior beauty in "Puella Mea":

> Harun Omar and Master Hafiz
> keep your dead beautiful ladies.

Mine is a little lovelier
than any of your ladies were. (*CP* 17)

Here, though, simple uniqueness rather than unique beauty is
what the lover focuses upon. If he credits his lady with some
of the traditional sonnet's graces—shy glance, fragile lips—he
admires as well "the very skilful strangeness of your smile/ the
keen primeval silence of your hair." There is emotional precision in these latter formulations, but not any conventional
measure of loveliness. The traditional mode, singing beauty
and virtue, appeals to common standards of taste and value; it
is public. Cummings' sweetest song is private, it embraces
simply the "perfectly alive."

Characteristic of him are a willingness to run poetic risk
and an originality in overcoming it; "if i have made" exemplifies both. Already for Shakespeare, the sonneteer's elaborate
praise had swelled to bathos—he pricked it in "My mistress'
eyes are nothing like the sun"—and Cummings, admiring his
lady's "eyes," "body," "glance," "smile," "hair," and "lips,"
daringly flirts with a three-hundred-year-old cliché. He avoids
it, however—building upon rather than imitating tradition—by
the ingenious and original use of language. Mixing the diction
of the Elizabethan sonnet with a sprinkling of words that con-
travene it, he stops us, nodding at an echo, short. We look
again and find the old phrase altered, the old praise refined.
The mood remains courtly, but the images—traditional simile
as well as radically implied metaphor—are fresh and haunting.

Line 7, "the very skilful strangeness of your smile," serves
as example. Yoking the technical and practiced suggestions of
"skilful" with the courtly and mysterious ones of "strangeness," Cummings achieves a complexity of connotation that
forces us to see the individuality of his lady. Avoiding cliché,
he slips the sonneteer's snare: *this* lady will not seem to us just
another paradigm of virtue and beauty. Her smile, like Mona
Lisa's, will stay with us. Similarly operative is "the keen primeval silence of your hair," where again suggestions precise

and technical complicate the mysterious and romantic. Such formulations defy paraphrase but, like Hart Crane's "logic of metaphor"—which Cummings knew and admired: "a true poet," he wrote, his highest praise (*L* 260)—they obviate the need for it. They have their own precisions, indelible, alive, highly specific.

They have a rich inventiveness as well, and we see it nowhere better than in the sonnet's final lines, "lady through whose profound and fragile lips/ the sweet small clumsy feet of April came/ into the ragged meadow of my soul." The implied metaphor of these lines describes a birth, the fulfilled labor of creation: child April, wobbly and delicate as a new-born colt, enters the world and the speaker's consciousness. The birth itself, however, is metaphoric, for April—the poem's crucial, only capitalized word—is more than child or season. It is a state of mind, a condition of grace. Bringing first color to the "ragged meadow," April suggests kinetic life, perfect love— "april's where we're" declares the deliciously expectant lover of a later poem (*CP* 578)—and needed salvation. Before April, the poet-speaker's soul was a ragged meadow. After it, demur though he may about his song's success, that singer takes on some of the hum of harmony, the perfect aliveness of his lady.

"in Just-" (CP 24)

in Just-
spring   when the world is mud-
luscious the little
lame balloonman

whistles   far   and wee

and eddieandbill come
running from marbles and
piracies and it's
spring

when the world is puddle-wonderful

the queer
old balloonman whistles
far   and   wee
and bettyandisbel come dancing

from hop-scotch and jump-rope and

it's
spring
and
    the

        goat-footed

balloonMan   whistles
far
and
wee

Our language has no verb to describe the process that follows winter. Justly celebrated, "in Just-/ spring" is a charming,
vivacious attempt to supply one. Cummings tells no story here,
makes no judgment; instead, he captures the emotional nu-
ances of seasonal rebirth in a single lyric impression, an aesthetic equivalent for feelings that is so precise and so unified it
informs our consciousness with the authority of a new word.
Like Dr. Williams' wonderful "By the road to the contagious
hospital,"[10] Cummings' entire poem routs the fixity of an
English noun, stirs it to linguistic and therefore cognitive motion; almost literally, the poet verbalizes spring.

    Catalyst of the process is a goat-footed, whistling balloon-
man, the essence of two Pans. Like Peter, he is the spokesman
of wish. His helium balloons, defying gravity as children and
poets should, suggest dreams: hold on to them, like the wish-
kite of "o by the by" (*CP* 593), and be carried up to never-never
(Cummings would say always-possible) land; for

      who knows if the moon's
      a balloon,coming out of a keen city
      in the sky . . .

```
             . . . where
          always
             it's
          Spring . . . (CP 129)
```

Like the satyr-god, with the lecherous goat's torso and the legendary skill at piping, the balloonman epitomizes fertility. Bringing the sexually separate children together—"eddieandbill come/ running from marbles and/ piracies," "bettyandisbel . . . // from hop-scotch and jump-rope"—he is the divine maypole about which these innocents begin *le sacre du printemps*, the rhythmic dance that will ensure continued human springs.

The dance image is not far-fetched, for, witty even in structure, Cummings uses a musical rondo form to evoke the season's cyclic return. There are five sections to his poem, and its *ababa* pattern—lines 1–5, 9–13, and 17–22 are the *a* sections, 6–8 and 14–16 the *b*—neatly echoes the subject. The main theme is just-spring, that instant when the earth turns once again to life, and its exposition follows the balloon-carrying harbinger through his tonic whistle. Measured but lively—only the poem's special, spatial art can reproduce the exact vocal cadence here—the tune slows at spondaic "Just-/ spring" and "mud-/ luscious," lilts at the anapestic "when the world." In sharp musical contrast is the pell-mell second theme, a tumble of children: "and eddieandbill come/ running from marbles and/ piracies and it's/ spring." Unleashed energies explode in this rush; not only the slurred names but even grammatical structure, unsubordinative in its flurry of "and"s, sound the excitement. With the held note "spring," a *ritardando*, the haste of the *b* section is checked and *a* resumes. Again this theme is measured but not confined: its pace is slowed by the different vowels emphasized—i, û, u-u, ē, ō, ōō, i, ä, ē—but the liveliness of "puddle-wonderful" precludes solemnity. The second *b* introduces *staccato*, neatly underscoring it with stopped consonants—"bettyandisbel come dancing// from hop-scotch and jump-rope"—while the final section returns for a last, lingering look at the main theme.

Nothing is haphazard here, everything functions. What seems at first mere idiosyncracy quickly reveals itself to be a kind of notation, like the musical rest; using the white space within or between lines, Cummings is able to regulate the poem's tempo. He can distinguish, for example, between "far   and wee," the balloonman's initial, approaching whistle, and "far/ and/ wee," his final, valedictory one; he can lengthen the last statement of the main theme, shorn now of its description of earth, to equal in time its earlier expositions. Similarly functional is the lack of period, comma, and the like. The poet avoids grammatical stops because the season he describes runs like a watercolor; punctuation, regimenting phrase and clause, would delineate too sharply for this mud-luscious time. Without it, line flows into line, modifiers double and overlap. We gain an impression of spring's coursing life, while the thread of sense is never lost.

"may i feel said he" (CP 399)

may i feel said he
(i'll squeal said she
just once said he)
it's fun said she

(may i touch said he
how much said she
a lot said he)
why not said she

(let's go said he
not too far said she
what's too far said he
where you are said she)

may i stay said he
(which way said she
like this said he
if you kiss said she

may i move said he
is it love said she)
if you're willing said he
(but you're killing said she

but it's life said he
but your wife said she
now said he)
ow said she

(tiptop said he
don't stop said she
oh no said he)
go slow said she

(cccome?said he
ummm said she)
you're divine!said he
(you are Mine said she)

The fun of E. E. Cummings—his everpresent wit, his delight in unorthodoxy and invention, his cheerful uninhibited-ness—is a gift our rather somber century should rejoice in. Occasionally, however, readers slight it; embracing Cummings the bitter satirist and Cummings the courtly lover, they reject the maker of light and playful verse. In doing so, they miss a kind of master. For though Cummings' best poems lie outside the proper boundaries of this category, his best poems within it have a verve and grace entirely their own. Matthew Arnold preferred Shakespeare to Chaucer, and we are apt to find "my father moved through dooms of love" a better poem than "she being Brand." Yet who is so highly serious that he cannot enjoy an occasional flippant moment? Relax our stern expecta-tions about poetry, enter gaily the world of lighter verse, and we may find a Cummings nearly as rewarding as the satirist and lover. We may find, too, inklings of seriousness in the midst of the most ribald comedy.

A case in point is the poem "may i feel said he." This straightforward little dramatic dialogue, the conversation sur-rounding an apparently casual sexual encounter, poses few outright difficulties. Yet it may be highly implicative. Examine it with an ear to hints of seriousness as well as obvious humor, and we will catch resonances far more interesting than those of the gramophone by the typist's divan. For here is no waste land: "he" and "she" may be archetypal male and female, but as the poem choreographs the whole of their sexual dance, from prelude to last lingering chords, they move through playful lust to a measure of grace. If Cummings pokes gentle fun at the physicality of his hero and the possessiveness of his heroine, he mixes it with affection. If the encounter seems almost indiscriminate, let us note that its close posits a communion no less meaningful for the bedroom clichés of its participants. There is, in short, cooperation here, interdependence, surrender —a kind of love. While the words of the characters are a secular litany chanted to ward off social discord, their actions imply fundamental harmony. "He" and "she" are less serious, more bawdy, and less developed characters than heroic "anyone" and "noone" (*CP* 515), but perhaps they share a place in Cummings' vision. Like "Brave" (Ares-Mars) and "Beautiful" (Aphrodite-Venus), at bottom they care nothing for the social contract. In a world where "reason [has] vanquished instinct and/ matter bec[o]me a slave of mind" (*CP* 799), they strike a blow for life, not logic.

Technique here is careful, conscious, and rather clever, the poem's simplicity notwithstanding. Form, for example, is highly expressive. The brevity of the dimeter lines and the repeated pattern, ". . . he said/ . . . she said," generate an air of inevitability. This is amplified by the rhythmic, responsory nature of the dialogue—a line at a time, "he" and "she" alternate their way through the ceremony of seduction—and by the weight of rhyme on key words. Rhyme, indeed, marks the compacted essence of this game of love—

> feel?
> squeal.
> once?
> fun!

touch?
much?
a lot.
why not?!

—and in its insistent ring we may hear almost the note of ritual.
Yet the ritual is not, like that of the "how town" 's passive
inhabitants, sterile. There,

someones married their everyones
laughed their cryings and did their dance
(sleep wake hope and then)they
said their nevers they slept their dream. (*CP* 515)

Here we have action and passion, a liveliness neatly echoed by
the form. Thus when the poem's lady offers her initial objec-
tion—"may i feel said he/ (i'll squeal said she"—the rhyme
suggests that agreement may underlie the temporarily discord-
ant vocal surface. Indeed, just as the entire process, verbal spar-
ring to triumphant aftermath, is an integral part of the sexual
dance, so from the very outset the orderly alternation of dialogue implies a harmony that comes of tension, the push and
pull of love. Even parentheses, seemingly haphazard, mirror
rhythm and significance. Rising and falling—first 2 lines are
enclosed, then 3, 4, 5, 4, 3, 2, and 1—they are a visual image of
the sexual act: symmetrical, they culminate in unity.

"yes is a pleasant country:" (CP 578)

yes is a pleasant country:
if's wintry
(my lovely)
let's open the year

both is the very weather
(not either)
my treasure,
when violets appear

> love is a deeper season
> than reason;
> my sweet one
> (and april's where we're)

The cartographic metaphor is Yeats's—"That is no country for old men," he wrote, "The young/ In one another's arms, birds in the trees"[11]—but Cummings' map of the sensual realm emphasizes different boundaries. Yeats spoke for "Monuments of unaging intellect" against the sensual music of "Whatever is begotten, born, and dies"; Cummings sings the warmth of instinctual affirmation against the chill of reason. In the little cavalier poem "yes is a pleasant country:," he adds an interesting turn not only to Yeats's metaphor, but to the whole classical *carpe diem* situation.

The male speaker, addressing "my lovely," "my treasure," and "my sweet one," seems to respond to the lady's dampening "if." He puts his persuasion into three parallel stanzas, each a little plea that distinguishes by metaphor between the joy of surrender and the coolness of caution. In the first stanza, the "pleasant country" of "yes" is opposed to "if" 's "wintry" realm, and the self-evident force of the comparison evokes a metaphoric proposition, "let's open the year." This last gives interest to the poem: no traditional spring, whose weather, turning a young man's fancy, fathers love, this spring is instead fathered *by* love; in Cummings' universe the mutual surrender of two people is an act of such transcendent importance that it governs, rather than is governed by, the external world.

The same twist informs stanza two, where "both" and "either," the good weather of togetherness and the bad of separation, are contrasted. Strategically dropping the imperative "let's" of stanza one, the speaker here offers a statement so irresistible of implication that formal persuasion is unnecessary: two people at one with each other, unencumbered by dissociating "if"s, are truly alive; the flowering of their love makes any weather spring. The final stanza, incrementally repetitive, summarizes the earlier arguments by linking "yes" and "both," "if" and "either," to their generative roots, the "love" and "reason" that are positive and negative poles of Cummings' world. Confident now that the day will be seized, the persuasive lover concludes with a declaration of interdependence: not only is abstract "love . . . a deeper season/ than reason," but these particular two are in it, "april's where we're)."

Thus in three parallel stanzas of increasing rhetorical subtlety, the poem and its lovers move from the relative uncertainty that cajoling proposition implies to the delicious expectation of fulfillment. Two technical devices quietly foster this movement, rhyme and the use of parentheses. We hardly notice the *aaab cccb dddb* rhyme scheme, because the triplets are feminine and imperfect: "country," "wintry," "lovely"; "weather," "either," "treasure"; "season," "reason," "sweet one." But this down-playing is functional: it emphasizes by contrast the exact, masculine rhymes of the fourth, eighth, and twelfth lines, "year," "appear," "we're," which link the stanzas and draw attention to their parallelism. This is particularly effective here because each stanza's concluding line makes or completes a metaphoric or implied proposition, and so the exact rhyme, calling up earlier proposals, drums away resistance.

Parentheses, not unifying here, point to development. The first stanza's direct address to "(my lovely)" is an eye-twinkling but rhetorically underplayed aside, toned down by parentheses so that the speaker, uncertain about the girl's response, may seem merely to generalize. Increasingly confident in stanza two, he no longer hesitates to address her, but, persuasively emphasizing the positive, plays down instead the undesired alternative, "(not either)." In the final stanza the expectant lover, eyes twinkling again, subdues only his outright declaration, "(and april's where we're)," lest perhaps he seem *too* sure. Development is clear here, and the next stanza, needing no parentheses, needs no words either.

3

SO MANY SELVES

It is not what I eat that is
my natural meat,
the hero says. He's not out
seeing a sight but the rock
crystal thing to see—the startling El Greco
brimming with inner light—that
covets nothing that it has let go.

—Marianne Moore,
"*The Hero*"

"o by the by" (CP 593)

o by the by
has anybody seen
little you-i
who stood on a green
hill and threw
his wish at blue

with a swoop and a dart
out flew his wish
(it dived like a fish
but it climbed like a dream)
throbbing like a heart
singing like a flame

blue took it my
far beyond far
and high beyond high
bluer took it your
but bluest took it our
away beyond where

what a wonderful thing
is the end of a string
(murmurs little you-i
as the hill becomes nil)
and will somebody tell
me why people let go

Like Frost, Cummings was a metaphysical poet, one eager
to get beyond the seen world into the unseen. Frost, though,
had always promises to keep, a deep and final love for the par-
ticularities of human existence that outweighed divine tempta-
tion. "I'd like to get away from earth awhile," he tells us, but
—crucially—"then come back to it and begin over": "Earth's
the right place for love:/ I don't know where it's likely to go
better."[1] Cummings' faith goes the other way. Loyal as he is
to the mysteries of "sweet spontaneous/ earth" (CP 46), his

holiest vows are to the land of dreams. Thus his heroes—his many selves—walk our world proudly and humbly apart from most men. Alert to timely joys—to Christmas trees, "Your smile/ eyes knees and . . . your Etcetera" (*CP* 276)— they are most alive to the perfect vision behind those joys, to the cyclic return of spring and the limitlessness of love. In Frost, lush red apples physically separate earth's green and the blue of sky, mediate between metaphysical planes; luring the poet to satiety, they yet hold him in the land's thrall.[2] Cummings' "o by the by" lacks such a stay. Standing "on a green/ hill," the poem's Platonically whole hero, little you-i, "[throws] his wish at blue." Decisively, he embraces dreams.

The poem's chief attraction owes much to Cummings the painter. It lies in an emblematic habit of mind, a graphic conception of metaphor. Like Herbert's "The Pulley" and "The Collar," distinguished predecessors in this genre, "o by the by" is based on an implied picture, a tableau that illustrates and underlines its thematic point.[3] Little you-i, the more than nominal conjunction of two lovers into a single flesh, throws aloft a wish that becomes a kite, then watches it rise: up for the single dream of the young man ("far beyond far"), higher for that of his lady ("high beyond high"), but entirely out of the world of dimensions for the shared dream of the two ("away beyond where"). In the picture, the wish-kite rises toward transcendence; you-i, joyfully holding its string, soars after it as the landscape becomes a diminished thing. Cummings' point is two-fold. Only through the mutual surrender of love can the individual fulfill himself—"one's not half two. It's two are halves of one:" (*CP* 556)—but that fulfillment is utterly transcendent. "As the hill becomes nil," you-i leaves the confinement of conventional reality and enters the "keen city" of dream, where "everyone's/ in love and flowers pick themselves" (*CP* 129).

In spirit, the poem is "L'Allegro" to the "Il Penseroso" of "Tears Eliot" (*L* 93); counterpoising "The Love Song of J. Alfred Prufrock," it is an answer to Eliot's fastidious pessimism. Vanished from earth, Cummings' you-i may remind us by association—"Let us go then, you and I"[4]—of the sadly present Prufrock; the two poems follow precisely antithetical paths. In "Prufrock," we descend through hazes of fog and pipe smoke to an ironic underworld, "Till human voices wake us and we drown." You-i, rising through clear air, soars toward transcendence. Prufrock, self-consciously observing the decay of his desires, wonders obsessively "would it have been worth while?" You-i, impulsively grasping his dream, wonders "why people let go." Prufrock, in short, has lacked the selfhood and the courage to "[squeeze] the universe into a ball/ To roll it towards some overwhelming question." You-i has dared that question—and gaily watched the ball of the earth fall away.

"i sing of Olaf glad and big" (CP 339)

i sing of Olaf glad and big
whose warmest heart recoiled at war:
a conscientious object-or

his wellbelovéd colonel(trig
westpointer most succintly bred)
took erring Olaf soon in hand;
but—though an host of overjoyed
noncoms(first knocking on the head
him)do through icy waters roll
that helplessness which others stroke
with brushes recently employed
anent this muddy toiletbowl,
while kindred intellects evoke
allegiance per blunt instruments—
Olaf(being to all intents
a corpse and wanting any rag
upon what God unto him gave)
responds,without getting annoyed
"I will not kiss your fucking flag"

I Am—A Study of E. E. Cummings' Poems

straightway the silver bird looked grave
(departing hurriedly to shave)

but—though all kinds of officers
(a yearning nation's blueeyed pride)
their passive prey did kick and curse
until for wear their clarion
voices and boots were much the worse,
and egged the firstclassprivates on
his rectum wickedly to tease
by means of skilfully applied
bayonets roasted hot with heat—
Olaf(upon what were once knees)
does almost ceaselessly repeat
"there is some shit I will not eat"

our president,being of which
assertions duly notified
threw the yellowsonofabitch
into a dungeon,where he died

Christ(of His mercy infinite)
i pray to see;and Olaf,too

preponderatingly because
unless statistics lie he was
more brave than me:more blond than you.

"Arma virumque" sang Vergil, beginning an epic distinguished for its civility; Cummings, adopting and adapting that
classical form, sings the man alone. The difference is implicative of both the spirit and the art of Cummings' poem. Olaf
embraces an integrity of private rather than public convictions;
acknowledging only his personal sense of truth rather than
merging his will with the gods', he is a veritable anti-Aeneas,
a new kind of hero. His poem, "i sing of Olaf glad and big,"
neatly reverses classical expectation by a series of ironic twists.
It is a small new epic, but one that accumulates considerable
power despite its formal miniature.

From the outset, the poem's force resides primarily in its

play upon heroic tradition. We learn not "the anger of Peleus' son Achilleus/ and its destruction" (Lattimore's translation), but the gentleness of Olaf, "whose warmest heart recoiled at war"; big and blond, our hero may be the physical image of the Germanic warrior, but his temperament is otherwise. The form does not undercut heroism—we do not deal here with mock epic—it instead offers alternative heroic values. In the *Iliad*, Achilles is a hero of physical strength, sulking like a child when Briseis is taken from him, but at last achieving immortality by slaughtering Trojans. Olaf's strength is moral. Scarcely annoyed as his self-righteous and sadistic torturers attempt to strip him of human dignity, he achieves epic stature by *refusing* to kill.

The shift has important implications. Heroic epic, from the *Iliad* to the *Chanson de Roland*, is based on communal values; a hero's greatness is a measure of the degree to which he exemplifies the qualities his society most prizes. With Olaf it is different. He must give up not merely his life but also the good name that valiance customarily wins, the hero's renown and reputation, υλέος. He can do so lightly, however, defying both the military force of his nation and its massively conformed opinions, because he answers to an individual rather than a collective truth, to personal vision rather than social regard.

Cummings' instrument of truth here is irony. From the beginning of the poem to the underplayed tribute of its final lines, we are led to ponder the relationship between what things seem and what they are. Thus, "recoiled," suggesting not the jump of a fired gun but the heart's horrified reaction to it, offers an initial perspective on the matter of war, flicks the first stone at traditional heroic glory. As the irony gathers, Cummings unmasks the modern bankruptcy of collective values. In a society so perverted that torture has become socially correct—it is administered by the "wellbelovéd colonel(trig/ westpointer most succinctly bred)"—sometimes only profanity can express the sacred heart. Refusing to "kiss your fucking flag,"[5] Olaf avoids the polite Latin that in our century has time and again been used to justify atrocity. His taut Anglo-Saxon, direct as his behavior, is comment enough on his suave persecutors.

The ironies of the poem, then, sadly fulfill the implication of its early wordplay: conscientiously nonviolent Olaf has indeed become an "object" to the soulless torturers that surround him. In response to his love—the essence of nonviolence—he is beaten; in the face of his courage, "our president" finds him a "yellowsonofabitch." Yet the poem has greater impact than the customary moral fable. Cummings' laconic conclusion—a touch of Auden that Auden himself would use a few years later in "The Unknown Citizen"—forces us to deeper involvement than the approving nod. Its unusual comparison of hero with poet and reader—"unless statistics lie he was/ more brave than me: more blond than you"—suddenly strips away the comfortable distance that a morally simple struggle has erected for us. The speaker's irony in adopting the yardstick of Olaf's murderers, his invocation not of the muse—the visionary heart's truth—but of statistics, democracy's lowest common denominator, compels us to attend the casual equation of blondness and bravery, requires us not only to distinguish but to choose between appearance and reality; and the poem's stark duality leaves no room for middling heroics. Thus at the close we are denied the aristocratic pleasure of being an audience to epic, are instead thrown into the simple dramatic world of the form itself. We cannot reflectively sit in judgment, but are moved to ask uncomfortable—and perhaps life-giving—questions about ourselves.

"my father moved through dooms of love" (CP 520)

my father moved through dooms of love
through sames of am through haves of give,

singing each morning out of each night
my father moved through depths of height

this motionless forgetful where
turned at his glance to shining here;
that if(so timid air is firm)
under his eyes would stir and squirm

newly as from unburied which
floats the first who,his april touch
drove sleeping selves to swarm their fates
woke dreamers to their ghostly roots

and should some why completely weep
my father's fingers brought her sleep:
vainly no smallest voice might cry
for he could feel the mountains grow.

Lifting the valleys of the sea
my father moved through griefs of joy;
praising a forehead called the moon
singing desire into begin

joy was his song and joy so pure
a heart of star by him could steer
and pure so now and now so yes
the wrists of twilight would rejoice

keen as midsummer's keen beyond
conceiving mind of sun will stand,
so strictly(over utmost him
so hugely)stood my father's dream

his flesh was flesh his blood was blood:
no hungry man but wished him food;
no cripple wouldn't creep one mile
uphill to only see him smile.

Scorning the pomp of must and shall
my father moved through dooms of feel;
his anger was as right as rain
his pity was as green as grain

septembering arms of year extend
less humbly wealth to foe and friend
than he to foolish and to wise
offered immeasurable is

proudly and(by octobering flame
beckoned)as earth will downward climb,
so naked for immortal work
his shoulders marched against the dark

his sorrow was as true as bread:
no liar looked him in the head;
if every friend became his foe
he'd laugh and build a world with snow.

My father moved through theys of we,
singing each new leaf out of each tree
(and every child was sure that spring
danced when she heard my father sing)

then let men kill which cannot share,
let blood and flesh be mud and mire,
scheming imagine,passion willed,
freedom a drug that's bought and sold

giving to steal and cruel kind,
a heart to fear, to doubt a mind,
to differ a disease of same,
conform the pinnacle of am

though dull were all we taste as bright,
bitter all utterly things sweet,
maggoty minus and dumb death
all we inherit,all bequeath

and nothing quite so least as truth
—i say though hate were why men breathe—
because my father lived his soul
love is the whole and more than all

Cummings, whose independent ways baffled and threat-
ened the conservative, bucked the liberal deification of Freud as
well: he loved his father. "A New Hampshireman,"

6 foot 2, a crack shot & a famous fly-fisherman & a first-rate sailor . . . & a woodsman who could find his way through forests primeval without a compass & a canoe-ist who'd stillpaddle you up to a deer without ruffling the surface of a pond & an ornithologist & taxidermist & . . . an expert photographer (the best I've ever seen) & an actor . . . & a painter . . . & a better carpenter than any professional & an architect who designed his own houses before building them . . . & (while at Harvard) a teacher with small use for professors,[6]

the Reverend Edward Cummings was shaping ideal to his son. "My father moved through dooms of love," an elegiac remembrance, pays him tribute. No ceremonious procession from the bleakness of grief to a measure of found consolation, this poem is celebrative from the start. For in the courageous, creative joy of his father, Cummings feels a living presence, one that defeats not merely physical extinction but even the spiritual suicide of a world.

Perhaps it is no accident that Cummings, always a lover of the unexpected twist, should echo here the verse form of A. E. Housman. Like "To an Athlete Dying Young," "my father moved" is in iambic tetrameter quatrains, rhymed *aabb* (the form is rare for the American), but the two elegies could scarcely be farther apart in tone. Cummings was fond of Pound's "immortal parody" (*L* 234)—

> London is a woeful place,
> Shropshire is much pleasanter.
> Then let us smile a little space
> Upon fond nature's morbid grace.
> *Oh, Woe, woe, woe, etcetera. . . .*[7]

—and his own choice of form here is a parodic rebuttal of Housman's *Weltschmertz*. Not for Cummings' father, not for any hero in his universe, is Housman's desolate cry, "I, a stranger and afraid/ In a world I never made."[8] Cummings' adamic heroes are fearlessly native: with his joyous father as with Wallace Stevens' woman of imagination, "there never was a world for [him]/ Except the one [he] sang and, singing, made."[9]

Structurally, the poem falls into two parts, or, perhaps, sonata allegro form. In either case, stanzas 1–13 present and characterize "my father"—1–4 might be called exposition, 5–12 development, and 13, echoing 1, a brief recapitulation—while 14–17, a kind of coda, express the significance of his life. The poem, unusually long for Cummings, is syntactically tricky; it will be useful, then, to paraphrase the initial section, to show through a line-by-line consideration exactly how Cummings' language works. The devices thereby elucidated should make the rest of the syntax accessible and allow us to concentrate for the remaining sections on other aspects of the poetry.

The analogy with musical form is lent credence from the beginning, for father, like Orpheus, sings "each morning out of each night." Beyond Orpheus even, he is the all-creating God of Genesis, who transformed ("turned") things in general when in particular he set spinning ("turned") the vivid earth ("shining here") out of a still and formless void ("this motionless forgetful where"). "Moved through," which means "travelled amidst," "passed beyond," "was animated by," and "expressed himself by means of" (as God moved through the whirlwind), fosters the grand scale, while "dooms of love," "sames of am," "haves of give," and "depths of height," defined by opposition, suggest cosmic proportions. Embodying emotional rather than quantitative precision, emphasizing magnitude by suggesting all-inclusiveness, these strange formulations are poetically exact: oxymoronic qualities are peculiarly fitting to a force than can miraculously make "if," the passive and merely possible, "stir and squirm," that can transform the "timid . . . firm" air of calm-before-storm into active reality.

"Newly as from unburied which/ floats the first who," a difficult structure, is adverbial clause modifying "drove" and "woke": as "newly" as the personal "first who" floats out of the inanimate "unburied which"—hence as gently yet eagerly as possible—does father's "april touch" work. "Sleeping selves," passively nodding, are driven to actively "swarm their fates"; "dreamers"—the possibility is every man's, but is nearly everywhere in chains—are awakened to roots mysterious and spirittual, "ghostly" adding the Germanic sense of *geist* to its English mystery. In the next stanza, a weeping and abstract lady, "why"—her name suggests the sorrow-bringing need for explanations rather than the spontaneous embrace of intuition —receives the compassion of father's clearly unabstract "fingers." Able to comfort as well as drive, put to sleep as well as awaken, he is so intuitively in touch with all life—"he could feel the mountains grow"—that no tiniest voice escapes him. "Vainly," a pun, invokes both of father's capacities: the helpless will not cry in vain, nor will the vain go undetected.

The development section follows the exposition's linguistic shorthand, often bypassing denotation for the heft alone, the aura or charge, of words. Its images rarely define a specific area of transformation—they do not, like Macbeth, reduce life to a walking shadow—but they develop a cumulative power nevertheless. Thus whatever the parallel clauses that modify him mean, father in stanza 5 is active celebrant. "Lifting," "praising," "singing," whether of "sea," "moon," or the "desire" that was in their beginning, he conceives the universe to be organically whole, is in perfect harmony with it all. "Praising a forehead called the moon," he is moved by joy; "singing desire into begin," he is mover as well.

This is divinity in man, chanting a "boisterous devotion to the sun,/ Not as a god, but as a god might be,/ Naked . . . like a savage source."[10] Transcending the scrupulous shadows of the rational like "midsummer's keen[ness] of sun," the joyous song of feeling aligns father with the earth. More humbly than September trees offer their leaves to all, does father offer the qualitative rather than quantitative reality of self, "immeasurable is," to foolish and wise. His is the proud humility of open heart and simple liveliness, his "the heavenly fellowship/ Of men that perish and of summer morn."[11]

Yet a timeless salvation lodges in this specifically mortal triumph. Conveying the synergy of love, the coda rises to a stirring affirmation. Stupidity and cruelty, fear and hate, may turn the visible world inside out, but "What matter?"[12] Cummings' faith, no simpler than the tragic joy of Yeats, rests on the redemptive power of loving action. Father "lived his soul," and doing so experienced a creative joy that cannot vanish. Things inhabit a shadowy world, but the Platonic reality behind active love is immortal: "No handiwork of Callimachus" remains and "All things fall," but "those that build them again are gay."[13] Building, loving, acting: these are the province of a man, and he who dwells there need never be mourned.

Technically, the poem pivots upon several devices characteristic of Cummings. In the exposition, new nouns are created from old adverbs, adjectives, verbs, and pronouns, as Cummings stirs words into movements we have not seen them make before. The process is not invariably successful—it can be precious rather than lively—but now and then it achieves something dazzling: though the poem's second stanza will not replace the account of creation in Genesis, when "this motionless forgetful where/ turned at his glance to shining here," Cummings has come close, I think, to fleshing the λόγος before our very eyes. The development section continues such reconstitution of language by molding more of these images. Some, as suggested earlier, have almost wholly connotative meanings. Others reverse expectation in a form of hyperbole, as when father's joy is so pure that "a heart of star," essence of the mariner's trusted reference point, "by him could steer." The coda, in musical fashion, essays *bravura*. A *crescendo* of parallel structure grows, while the once-stated "let" and "be" beat, line upon line, with the controlled insistence of tympany. Everything rises to the *fortissimo* chant of the final couplet; music and intensity as well as structure and sense here emphasize a final resolution.

Yet the sweep of the poem comes from small things too. "Which" instead of "who" in stanza 14—"then let men kill which cannot share"—is a touch of precision as telling as Yeats's "the" for "his" in the final line of "Leda and the Swan"; it strips the humanity of its referrents as effectively as Yeats undercuts the fulfilled Zeus' energy. Even the length of vowels can be decisive here. When Cummings writes, "Scorning the pomp of must and shall/ my father moved through dooms of feel," there is of course the weight of meaning to his statement. But there is more. The shortness of the vowels in "pomp," "must," and "shall" emphasizes the triviality and meaninglessness of these things in contrast to the held sounds of "moved," "dooms," and "feel." This is art, not ingenuity. These lines are at the exact center of the poem. In their marriage of the musical and symbolic facets of language, they are its very heart indeed.

"sonnet entitled how to run the world)" (CP 390)

A always don't there B being no such thing
for C can't casts no shadow D drink and

E eat of her voice in whose silence the music of spring
lives F feel opens but shuts understand
G gladly forget little having less

with every least each most remembering
H highest fly only the flag that's furled

(sestet entitled grass is flesh or swim
who can and bathe who must or any dream
means more than sleep as more than know means guess)

I item i immaculately owe
dying one life and will my rest to these

children building this rainman out of snow

Pitting the always possible Eden of individual freedom against the world-negating limitation of *isms*, the "sonnet entitled how to run the world)" directs us not to try. Fiercely independent, Cummings brooked no system; almost alone among the literary voices of the war years, he rejected both the paralyzing selflessness of Communism—*Eimi,* his journal of a trip to Russia, is prophetically clear on this point—and the bent to sloganizing mindlessness of "democ/ ra(caveat emptor)cy" (*CP* 549). Instead he stood solitary, a latter-day Adam whose disciplined will lifted him above concern for society's dicta and freed him to realize the personal potential of imagination and aspiration.

It is this potential that concerns us here, for, ironically precise in their step by step, *A–I* delineation, the not-so-easy-to-follow directions announce at once the impossibility of running, of controlling, the world. "Always don't," directs step *A*, "there B being no such thing/ for C can't casts no shadow"; never even try to run the world, says Cummings, for a world limited by freedom-destroying negations ceases to be real. There is, however, another meaning to "run the world." Even as one runs the gauntlet, testing courage by a defenseless exposure to experience, so he can run the world, totally immersing himself in life, courageously surrendering to love. It is this self-fulfilling way to run the world that the rest of the poem describes.

"D drink and/ E eat of her voice in whose silence the music of spring/ lives," the next instructions, prescribe love, and, by a subtly implied comparison, evoke her mysterious ecstasies; if "the music of spring" lives in her silence, how wonderful indeed must be her voice, how natural and fulfilling the eating and drinking of it![14] *F* and *G*, difficult of syntax, offer further directions to the would-be self. "Feel," a noun, "opens but shuts" understanding, because feeling is for Cummings both beginning and end of knowledge. "But," however, not only conjunction here but iffy, cautious, cerebral noun ("no ifs, buts, or maybes"), governs its own verb, "shuts." In this way it opposes and contrasts "feel," for while "feel opens" understanding, "but shuts" it. *G*, the most difficult step to make sense of, seems to suggest living in an always new, active present rather than a possessive, passive past: "gladly forget," says

Cummings, for the little we have is depleted still further by each bit of the inevitably unrecapturable past that we tie it to, by "every least[,] each most[,] remembering." "H highest fly only the flag that's furled" bids us display most proudly not the mass-produced, flowing banner of national unanimity but the "furled" or rolled-up flag of privacy and uniqueness.

The self-proclaimed sestet of this self-proclaimed sonnet continues in the same vein. "Grass is flesh,"recalling by inversion the Bible—"All flesh is grass" (Isaiah 40:6)—and by association Walt Whitman (whose adamic vision lies always back of Cummings), implies that earth is alive. Since immersion in this life is the single secret, the poet directs those of us who can to enter completely; not to do so, Puritanically cleanly perhaps, is merely to "bathe," motivated by an end, cramped for room, and head out of water. Restating that "grass is flesh" and swimming beats bathing, Cummings explains that "any dream/means more than sleep as more than know means guess"; for "dream," an active, fantastic process, is as far beyond sleep's passive state as "guess," uncertain and alive, is beyond solid, dead, cerebral "know." I, the appropriate concluding step of an individualistic poem, is the willing and testamental victory of kinetic over static. The Cummingsean "i," immaculate not of dirt but of death-in-life (he swims rather than bathes), owes "one life" to "dying," because that process, operating usually on walking dead with unlived lives to give, finds here the cupboard bare, the life wholly used. The "rest" he wills, suggesting relaxation and remains, is actually neither: kinetic "i" is always in motion and children have no need for corpses. Instead, it is those ideals that have informed his life and live on after him, imagination and aspiration, a single, sufficient legacy. And "these/ children building this rainman out of snow" show a sense for their heritage. Intuitively at home with the processive interplay of grass and flesh, they delight in building what must soon be transformed; accepting pre-consciously the change that makes growth possible, they sense and accept the "rainman" beneath their snowman's glaze.

The craft and art of this half-Petrarchan credo, difficult to isolate, deserves mention nevertheless. Alliteration, for example, linking steps and instructions ("A always," "B being," "C can't," ! . . "I item"), recreates the innocent world of mnemonic games ("A my name is Alan and my wife's name is Alice . . .") and leads us thence to the constructive fantasies of rainman-building children. So little a thing as the single, closing parenthesis of line 1, implying the restrictive, wrong way to run the world, has its effect. So too the rhyme scheme, which, neither Italian nor English here, is irregular but consequent: Cummings has carefully framed, by "world" and "furled," the octave, for in true Petrarchan fashion, a shift in focus follows it. Indeed, that very shift, from the general to the specific, the implied "you" of the octave's imperatives to the "i" of the sestet, underscores the thematic rejection of collective *isms* and the thematic embrace of the individual. And what form could be more appropriate to Cummings' theme than this violated sonnet? The poem tells us that the way of disciplined, imaginative freedom rather than that of life-destroying injunction is "how to run the world," and Cummings' light-hearted but conscious use of a fruitful tradition echoes this convincingly.

"so many selves(so many fiends and gods" (CP 609)

so many selves(so many fiends and gods
each greedier than every)is a man
(so easily one in another hides;
yet man can,being all,escape from none)

so huge a tumult is the simplest wish:
so pitiless a massacre the hope
most innocent(so deep's the mind of flesh
and so awake what waking calls asleep)

so never is most lonely man alone
(his briefest breathing lives some planet's year,

his longest life's a heartbeat of some sun;
his least unmotion roams the youngest star)

—how should a fool that calls him "I" presume
to comprehend not numerable whom?

Like Walt Whitman—like any poet, any man—Cummings
was large, he contained multitudes. Recognizing and accepting
this, he particularly admired those people who could integrate
the diverse facets of personality into a unity of being, who could
embody out of the variegated antinomies of the human psyche
an heroic ideal. Yet though much of Cummings' work is either
a celebration of such heroes or an angry denunciation of their
failed opposites, the poet is not, as sometimes supposed, ignorant of "All mere complexities,/ . . . the mire of human
veins."[15] He may incline to concentrate elsewhere, but poems
like "so many selves(so many fiends and gods" make clear
Cummings' familiarity with the relative's existential intrusion
on the absolute, his thorough acquaintance with "the foul rag-
and-bone shop of the heart."[16] He may emphasize the almost
perfected humanity of Olaf, of his father, or of little you-i, but
Cummings knew well the struggle that such divinity in man
resolved. Before love, a blessed rage for order, could triumph,
the poet saw that men must come to terms with the chaos of
their own contradictory impulses.

His attitude toward these impulses is characteristic: even
as we define, proudly humble, our position in a complex universe, we must take full responsibility for each smallest part
of ourselves. Like Pope, Cummings saw man "Plac'd on this
isthmus of a middle state,/ A being darkly wise, and rudely
great," but the American was never "In doubt to deem himself
a God, or Beast."[17] He saw clearly that man is both, "many
fiends and gods," and that, indeed, precisely this complexity
makes identity so crucial in his world. When "so huge a tumult is the simplest wish:/ so pitiless a massacre the hope/ most
innocent," special emphasis must be put upon the poet's first

commandment, "Know then thyself." And this responsibility is the point of Cummings' poem.

One may bear it falsely or truly. False is the way of self-importance, the egotism of the world's "someones" and "everyones." The capitalized "I" of such people, indicating not unity of being but a homocentricity at odds with every physical and metaphysical fact in our universe, allows the individual no individuality. Tying him to a mask, a persona, it costs him all knowledge of the selves that mask denies.[18] True is the way of self-discipline, the courageous exploration of everything in us, for only in this manner can we discover the roots of unity, the path toward that humble self-love that makes possible the heroic ideal. Thus the poem's final couplet—a rhetorical question whose emphatic answer is "He cannot!"—declares the symbolic import of the poet's lower-case "i": with it, Cummings reminds himself and us of man's need to avoid intellectual pride, his responsibility for open-heartedness. The fool's "I," in contrast —at issue, of course, is metaphor rather than typography—suggests a failed courage, a refusal to grow; the man who in Cummings' special sense calls himself "I" cannot begin to know of whom he speaks.

The technique of this simple, melodic poem scarcely requires comment, but we may note with interest the poet's choice of form. Typically, paradoxist Cummings is most traditional in defending his unorthodoxy. Thus, justifying the sometimes essential iconoclasm of the man who truly feels— and, on the poem's literal level, justifying as well a critical *cause célèbre*, the lower-case "i"—the poet conducts a strict Shakespearean sonnet in his defense. The choice is a good one. Allowing a certain latitude, like the effective consonantal rhyme of the quatrains here, the sonnet form's structural rigor and historic past help to establish the continuity of Cummings' values with those of other artists; for form is not a sack to be filled, but a subscription to aesthetic principles. Defining the individuality of his voice through traditional form, Cummings is lent not only grace, but authenticity as well.

4

DYING
IS
FINE

And this last blessing most,

    That the closer I move
To death, one man through his sundered hulks,
    The louder the sun blooms
And the tusked, ramshackling sea exults;
    And every wave of the way
And gale I tackle, the whole world then,
    With more triumphant faith
Than ever was since the world was said,
    Spins its morning of praise . . .

               —Dylan Thomas,
                 "Poem On His Birthday"

"when god lets my body be" (CP 16)

when god lets my body be

From each brave eye shall sprout a tree
fruit that dangles therefrom

the purpled world will dance upon
Between my lips which did sing

a rose shall beget the spring
that maidens whom passion wastes

will lay between their little breasts
My strong fingers beneath the snow

Into strenuous birds shall go
my love walking in the grass

their wings will touch with her face
and all the while shall my heart be

With the bulge and nuzzle of the sea

To be extinguished like a light, to become, like Buffalo
Bill, "defunct" (*CP* 60): such an end violates the transcendent
longings of the affirming soul. A poet, then, especially a romantic poet, must integrate the empirical certainty of stopped
hearts with his intuitive grasp of a wider permanence, must
broaden the territory of life to include death. William Wordsworth invoked the processive assertion that death forms but
part of a cycle—his dead Lucy "Neither hears nor sees," but,
"Rolled round in earth's diurnal course,/ With rocks, and
stones, and trees,"[1] she remains a part of Nature's grand design
—and young Dylan Thomas, windier, would chant a similar
unity:

Dead men naked they shall be one
With the man in the wind and the west moon;
When their bones are picked clean and the clean bones gone,
They shall have stars at elbow and foot.[2]

Death may be apprehended not as rigid finality but as sea change, not as end but as new beginning, and so seen, it "shall have no dominion." In the early poem "when god lets my body be," E. E. Cummings extends this salving doctrine of reintegration, embracing its physical tenets and combining them with a sensuous legacy of the soul. For Cummings, the organic unity of life and death is evident not merely in the transformation of one dust to another—however physically alive those dusts may be—but, more crucially, in a received bequest of vital spirit.

The poem offers no difficulties, only precisions of image, form, and language that move us toward its experience. Particularly effective is the treatment of transformation, for in combined "eye[s]," "lips," "fingers," and "heart"—the temples of romantic love—the speaker's spiritual essence is metamorphosed along with his flesh. Each change involves a correspondence, as if of related links on a chain of being: the shape of an "eye" resembles that of the seed from which "shall sprout a tree," the delicacy and color of "lips" ally them to roses, the vital motion of "strong fingers" suggests "strenuous birds," and the beating rhythm of "my heart" echoes "the sea." And each altered organ will continue, in its new form, the character of its old. Eyes that saw and rejoiced in the earth's beauty will now offer fruit to the lush, "purpled world"; lips that sang love's praise will as roses symbolize its transcendence; fingers that limned the beloved's form will as birds again "touch her face"; and beating heart will merge with tidal sea, the sources of love and life itself conjoin.

Form, too, helps in fusing life and death into a kinetic cycle that transcends their separation. The poem is a series of seven couplets, but Cummings, instead of isolating them and evoking the couplet's sense of self-containment, has separated rhyming lines. Paradoxically, this enables him to unite them more meaningfully. Linking stanzas rather than enclosing them, rhyme crosses the usual boundaries and thereby underscores the thematic connection between life and death. Further, the conventionally linear development of life is extended and given larger context by an unexpected, circular rhyme scheme, *a ab bc cd de ef fa a*; the romantic progression of "eye[s]," "lips," "fingers," and "heart" (this last a chivalric displacement) suggests physical consummation, and ultimately, therefore, being consumed, but the final couplet's return to an *a* rhyme rather than the expected *g* replenishes the flesh, prepares for another cycle. Repeating the rhyme word "be" and symmetrically isolating first and final lines, the poet emphasizes this return and its transcendent implications.

Linguistic precisions, more difficult in this poem to delineate than formal or imagistic ones, nevertheless deserve mention. Noteworthy is the way Cummings legitimizes his diction. In our century, we have come to suspect the vocabulary of sentiment employed here—"god," "brave," "tree," "fruit"; "dance," "lips," "sing," "rose"; "spring," "maidens," "passions," "breasts"; "snow," "birds," "love," "grass"; "wings," "touch," "heart," and "sea"— but Cummings mitigates that suspicion. Keeping his basic iambic tetrameter extremely flexible—there are only two or three regular lines in the poem's fourteen—he controls a supple and highly individual rhythm, one very different from the prosodic automatism with which a romantic diction is often paired. At the same time, the poet gives language his personal signature. The seemingly slack "lets ... be" of the very first line conceals a double meaning that unifies apparent antitheses, draws life and death together; for when god "lets my body be"—on the one hand withdraws from it the divine spark of life, on the other permits it continued existence—the speaker, medically dead, will live on. A phrase in the middle of the poem, "strenuous birds," extends the traditional diction of romance, bringing new connotation to a working adjective. Most original and effective, however, are the last line's splendid "bulge" and "nuzzle." Here, characteristically transforming language, Cummings tugs verbs into nominative service and moves the sea. His words, commingling suggestions of love and tide, evoke the perpetual freshness of eternal flux, not just of the ocean's cycle but of life's.

"All in green went my love riding" (CP 14)

All in green went my love riding
on a great horse of gold
into the silver dawn.

four lean hounds crouched low and smiling
the merry deer ran before.

Fleeter be they than dappled dreams
the swift sweet deer
the red rare deer.

Four red roebuck at a white water
the cruel bugle sang before.

Horn at hip went my love riding
riding the echo down
into the silver dawn.

four lean hounds crouched low and smiling
the level meadows ran before.

Softer be they than slippered sleep
the lean lithe deer
the fleet flown deer.

Four fleet does at a gold valley
the famished arrow sang before.

Bow at belt went my love riding
riding the mountain down
into the silver dawn.

four lean hounds crouched low and smiling
the sheer peaks ran before.

Paler be they than daunting death
the sleek slim deer
the tall tense deer.

Four tall stags at a green mountain
the lucky hunter sang before.

All in green went my love riding
on a great horse of gold
into the silver dawn.

four lean hounds crouched low and smiling
my heart fell dead before.

Cummings studied classical languages at Harvard, but like
Ezra Pound, whom he knew and admired, he spoke often in
his poems the medieval tongue of courtly love. Nowhere does
he weave more gracefully these threads ancient and merely old
than in the verbal tapestry "All in green went my love riding."
This luminous, initially perplexing poem is at last a statement
by example of one of Cummings' fundamental aesthetic beliefs.
Fusing the Diana and Actaeon legend with the medieval hunt,
bringing the resources of ballad and allegory to a uniquely expanded Shakespearean sonnet, the poem gathers at the inter-
section of beauty and terror. From the emotional vantage point
of that crossing—the poet achieves it through fourteen haunting tableaux, each at once distinct and implicative—we can in-
fer a good deal about the essence of tragedy and beauty, the
nature of passivity and action.

Myth enwrought seems substance here, the subject a lover's
dilemma. In Roman (and Greek) mythology, Diana (Arte-
mis), chaste goddess of the chase, protectress of wildlife, is
challenged by Actaeon, a famous but mortal hunter who feels
he can outshoot her. The goddess, whether directly for his
ὕβρις or because Actaeon is indeed the better marksman,
changes him into a stag. He feels fear for the first time, and
his hounds, sensing this, set upon and kill him. Adding romance to the myth—a courtly Diana here, loving the hunter,
is torn between the gentle beauty of the deer and the chivalric
flash of their pursuer—Cummings intensifies the fatal transformation toward which the action builds.

This poem is evidence—more profound evidence, I think,

than Cummings' celebrated quasi-ideograms—that the painting side of the man lived always with the poet. Dramatically visual, "All in green" suggests in its use of myth, its courtliness, and its spatial orientation a medieval tapestry. Each stanza is not merely self-contained—unusual for Cummings—each is primarily a picture. Thus we see emphasized the physical characteristics of the action—number, color, place—rather than the actors' states of mind. Thus, too, the word "before," ending seven of the fourteen stanzas, recurs: it offers visual perspective, the graphic layout. The painter's specificity, then, encompasses not merely concrete details, though these abound, it extends as well to composition; we see not only "four red roebuck at a white water" and the "cruel bugle," synecdochic hunter, but are shown also the relative positions of the antagonists, watering deer to the right, hunter at the left foreground. The whole technique is particularly useful in this poem because its frame effect, the suspense-creating discontinuity that forms and informs tapestry, leaps sudden as a clicked shutter to the hero's unexpected death.

Graphically conceived, the poem is nevertheless linear in structure. Its literal magic is prefigured and given context by the echo of ballad and allegory—by repetition and the miraculous, pregnant detail and narrative enigma[3]—and its poetic magic owes still more to the tightness of the Shakespearean sonnet. Indeed, if we consider each stanza an extended single line, "All in green" *is* such a sonnet. Thus we may divide it into three minutely parallel "quatrains" and a final, surprising "couplet." Told from Diana's point of view, the poem in its quatrains develops the increasingly difficult chase and presents the convergence of the speaker's conflicting sympathies; its couplet concentrates the fatal metamorphosis into a fine and final pun.

Specific lines offer little difficulty. Shortly after a courtly start—the "green," "gold," and "silver" of expanded line 1 might fancifully suggest medieval illumination—the poem becomes ominous with suggestive conflict. Line 2, juxtaposing odious hounds and "merry deer," sets sympathies as well as sides; line 3 underscores them. When "my love" is identified as a hunter by the "cruel bugle" of line 4, the dilemma's horns begin to sprout. With the second quatrain—the "horn at hip" is of course the preceding line's bugle—the hunt quickens. Ground shifts from "a white water" to "level meadows" and "a gold valley"; Diana's description of the deer trades the lightness of "dream" for more serious "sleep." No mere bugle now, the equipment of the chase is "the famished arrow." The final quatrain brings to a climax both chase and dilemma. The ground rises to "sheer peaks" and "a green mountain"; the tired deer, now within range, are "paler . . . than daunting death."

Yet the "lucky hunter" is attended by a complex irony that prefigures disaster. If he is lucky in anticipated success, it is that very success which will undo him. If he is lucky in the medieval sense of affection—"Ye gaif me lief, fair lucky dame" (*OED*)—at this crucial moment he will prove insufficiently dear to Diana. There is, then, a simple verbal irony too: for the couplet, cryptically spanning the hunt from start to finish —its first line repeats the poem's first—springs the news of Actaeon's death. Changed by the goddess into a hart, a red male deer, he is killed by his dogs. And so the final cry, "my heart fell dead before," concentrates Actaeon both as Diana's love and as metamorphosed deer, while conveying at the same time the lady's terrified swoon.

The implication of this allegoric hunt, the upshot of this mixture of sonnet and tapestry, linear exposition and graphic concept, lies in the poem's movement. From the outset we are caught in a dreamlike flux of color, landscape, even gender. In the half-light of dawn, "green," "gold," "silver," "red," and "white" flash past. Terrain alters, and even the deer change from "roebuck" to "does" to "stags." Static in this flux, an insistent refrain repeated once for each dog, are "four lean hounds crouched low and smiling." Unmoving, uncolored, they can kill others, but as Yeats, "a true poet" (*L* 188), had taught, they are themselves dead. For if

The horse that comes from the road,
The rider, the birds that range
From cloud to tumbling cloud,
Minute by minute they change,[4]

then these hounds, perpetually still in the midst of all, contradict the life-defining principle of kinesis.

Ultimately, "All in green" asserts the superiority of action to pulse-beat, dying to death-in-life. Diana and Actaeon both suffer a kind of death, but because their losses are sustained in passion rather than passivity, those deaths are life-giving. Literally, of course, their tragedy saves the deer; classically, however, and in the tradition of the sonnet, it perpetuates the lovers themselves, making their story memorable and fit for poetry. Cost what it must, Cummings tells us, action alone proves vital; in the vacuum of its absence, love—life—is sucked away. There is, then, beauty in tragedy, though a terrible beauty, because tragedy is active. Only the hounds here, crouched and colorless, neither move nor move *us*; stasis alone, in the world of E. E. Cummings, is immitigably ugly.

"suppose" (CP 102)

suppose
Life is an old man carrying flowers on his head.

young death sits in a café
smiling, a piece of money held between
his thumb and first finger

(i say "will he buy flowers" to you
and "Death is young
life wears velour trousers
life totters, life has a beard" i

say to you who are silent.—"Do you see
Life? he is there and here,
or that, or this

Dying Is Fine
63

or nothing or an old man 3 thirds
asleep, on his head
flowers, always crying
to nobody something about les
roses les bluets
        yes,
            will He buy?
Les belles bottes—oh hear
,pas chères")

and my love slowly answered I think so. But
I think I see someone else

there is a lady, whose name is Afterwards
she is sitting beside young death, is slender;
likes flowers.

"A great man in his pride"—the mature poet, say—"knows death to the bone."[5] The knowledge is hard won, though. Typically, the poet must grapple in his youth with the shattering personal recognition of death before he is able to understand—and accept or overcome—mortality. Cummings, I think, was no exception to this rule; "suppose," an early poem, records its speaker's frantic if imaginative efforts to come to terms with his own finitude. The poem suggests as well a good deal about its maker, for even as the young man who speaks it employs allegory to represent the emotional struggle raging within him, so Cummings seems to use the two personae of this dramatic dialogue to work out *his* internal conflict. There is import beyond the poem, then, for the gentle credo forged here: from the fire of conflict emerges no mere credible fiction, momentary stay against confusion, but a transcendental commitment that will mark indelibly the poet and his work.

Fear limits, hope transcends. As the young lover of "suppose" creates his allegorical Parisian café of existence, we see that, for all the imaginative potential his use of metaphor implies, he is at present too limited; amidst the café's seductive, ongoing hum, he notes only the negative terminal of a vital circuit. Thus for him life is "an old man 3 thirds/ asleep,"

while "young death . . . sits/ smiling"; down-and-out Life
carries flowers on his head, while flush Death, "a piece of
money held between/ his thumb and the first finger," prepares
to buy. The vision is linear: grounded in the logic of beginnings
and ends, it marks only the threat of nonexistence, the transfer
of flowers from Life to Death. And linear, it is incomplete, for
it fails to perceive this transfer's lively occasion, the transcendent lady Afterwards.

Tone is central to the understanding of this poem, and the
tonal contrast between lover and lady declaims as forcefully as
their words the difference in their outlooks. In the lover's dis-
junctive monologue, we hear a pessimism—

> "Death is young
> life wears velour trousers
> life totters, life has a beard"

—that rises toward fear:

> "Do you see
> Life? he is there and here,
> or that, or this
> or nothing or an old man 3 thirds
> asleep, on his head
> flowers, always crying
> to nobody something about les
> roses les bluets
>   yes,
>   will He buy?
> Les belles bottes—oh hear
> ,pas chères")

The lady's quiet, slow, and hopeful reply to this torrent offers
perspective:

> I think so. But
> I think I see someone else
>
> there is a lady, whose name is Afterwards
> she is sitting beside young death, is slender;
> likes flowers.

Dying Is Fine

65

Intuition understands, whereas perception merely knows; ontology sees precisely "all worlds" (*CP* 845) farther than empiricism. Fixing on condition rather than essence, on what will *happen* to the flowers rather than on the flowers themselves, this poem's noisily unhappy young man inhabits a world of frightening transience. His lady, "looking through both life and death" (*CP* 845), quietly touches something more central, more permanent, than either, the love and beauty that transcend condition.

It was neither an adolescent obsession nor a measure of Cummings' fondness for the Renaissance lyric that led the poet sometimes to depict death as a lover in his early poems. Love is a dying generation, a creation of new lives from old, and Cummings' grasp of this continuity made such a characterization both natural and expressive; though he focuses the metaphor differently, adding sexuality and altering gender, Cummings embraces Wallace Stevens' dictum, "Death is the mother of beauty."[6] Thus in "i like" (*CP* 42), the speaker's lady is entreated to receive death, if he come, "as your lover sumptuously/ being// kind," while in "O sweet spontaneous" (*CP* 46), death is the "rhythmic/ lover" of feminine earth, progenitor with her of spring.[7] In the present poem, Death emerges as the desiring lover of the lady Afterwards, though we must wait for the poem's close to learn this. The frightened initial speaker conceives the contrast between life and death to be one of weakness and strength, lassitude and vitality; young Death seems airily unattached, breezily unconcerned with the flowers of tottering life. Upon the expression of the lady's clearer vision, however, the initial contrast is refined. Death and life are seen to be parts of a cycle, each essential to the cycle's continuance. Life's flowers, a beauty seasonally recurrent and therefore eternal, are his essence, the distillation of his significance, and their sale to Death for the seduction of Afterwards suggests life's permanence rather than transience. "The body dies; the body's beauty lives," wrote Stevens;

So evenings die, in their green going,
A wave, interminably flowing.
So gardens die, their meek breath scenting
The cowl of winter, done repenting.
So maidens die, to the auroral
Celebration of a maiden's choral.[8]

Life moves inexorably toward death, but in that very movement is sown the regenerative seed. For though Death will lie
with the lady Afterwards, this defloration is in reality a celebration of flowers, a continuance of life's transcendent cycle.[9]

"dying is fine)but Death" (CP 604)

dying is fine)but Death

?o
baby
i

wouldn't like

Death if Death
were
good:for

when(instead of stopping to think)you

begin to feel of it,dying
's miraculous
why?be

cause dying is

perfectly natural;perfectly
putting
it mildly lively(but

Death

is strictly
scientific
& artificial &

evil & legal)

we thank thee
god
almighty for dying

(forgive us,o life!the sin of Death

Both metaphysical inclination and the didactic impulse drew Cummings to poetic techniques that surprise. The one helped him discover unexpected correspondences between temporal and eternal worlds, the other made him shock us into vision. His poetry is rich in examples of each, a physical if distant sphere expanding into an image of eternal dream in "who knows if the moon's/ a balloon" (*CP* 129), or a nursery rhyme turned nightmare in the atrocities of war:

some like it shot
and some like it hung
and some like it in the twot
nine months young (*CP* 497)

Sometimes, of course, this audacity becomes insulation, a coating of device that keeps us from the vital impulse of a poem; at its best, however, metaphysical audacity shortens the circuits of language and experience, conducting us straight to the source of current.

The crucial distinction in "dying is fine)but Death" exemplifies this effective metaphysics. The poem, Cummings' "Do not go gentle," rages not against the dying of the light but against an absence of liveliness, and the poet chooses linguistic difference to convey the force of this distinction. Uncapitalized "dying" hums with the sonic life of its voiced ending and the internal energy of its verbal origin; the gerund names but does not limit a kinetic process. "Death," on the other hand, a voiceless monosyllable self-importantly capitalized, is static noun. Cumming's entire poem develops the implications of these structural and grammatical differences, moving from the words themselves to the realities arrayed behind them.

At their simplest level, these realities involve "natural" and "scientific" attitudes about "Supersession of breath."[10] The natural man accepts death as part of a whole, a dynamic step in the miraculous process of being; unafraid, he feels it a mystery to be explored. The scientific man, though, isolates death by technical sanction—he measures, euphemizes, and permits it—and hopes thereby to minimize death's disturbing effects; frightened, he thinks it a mystery to be contained. On a more complex level, the realities behind "dying" and "Death" involve metaphoric extension. "Dying" comes to suggest an attitude about living, a joyful acceptance of the losses inevitably attendant upon growth. Indeed, on this plane of reality, living and dying are but two ways to name the same active process, for

> ...dying
>
> (as well as
> to cry and sing,
> my love
>
> and wonder)is something
>
> you have and i
> 've been
> doing as long as to
>
> (yes)forget(and longer
>
> dear... (CP 686)

We are born dying—blood, bones, and heart moving toward change—and to embrace this natural motion, to "begin to feel of it," is nothing less than to accept the gift of life. If, however, we reject this gift, we are condemned to stasis and reduced to finding virtue in our condemnation. This is the "Death" that man has created, "strictly/ scientific/ & artificial &/ evil & legal," a "stopping to think" that can paralyze the hearts of men whose electroencephalograms still show peaks and valleys. This is "the ὕβρις which is death's essence" (L 266), the fear to live that masquerades as power.

One need not hear Cummings' wonderful reading of "dying is fine"—though fortunately one can[11]—to hold the poem's rhetorical music in the mind's ear. From the start, rhythm makes the argument, beginning slowly for the first line's striking proposition, rapidly accelerating as the speaker warms to his subject, and then flexibly echoing the quality of the experience described. We have but to juxtapose the easy gait of "dying"—"perfectly natural; perfectly[,] putting it mildly[,] lively"—with the military march of "Death"—"strictly scientific & artificial & evil & legal"—to sense the poem's direction. When we oppose as well the flexible harmony of the first description with the drummed $\breve{\imath}$, $\bar{e}$, t, and l of the second—

strĭctly

scĭentĭfic

& artĭfĭcial &

ēvil & lēgal

—we begin to understand the care behind Cummings' art, the art behind his poetry.

"wild (at our first) beasts uttered human words" (CP 844)

> wild(at our first)beasts uttered human words
> —our second coming made stones sing like birds—
> but o the starhushed silence which our third's

Cummings was concerned with death from his first book of poems to his last, but during nearly fifty years of writing his feelings about it changed considerably. The early work, for all its affirmative vigor, understandably lacks the serenity that comes to a poet who has looked death in the eye and stared him down; the youthful Cummings may be defiant—"how do you like your blueeyed boy/ Mister Death" (*CP* 60)—or languorous—

                    if i believe
                    in death be sure
                    of this
                    it is

                    because you have loved me (*CP* 39)

—but the final ease of the confirmed visionary is wanting. Even a
fairly late poem, in which, "while all skies fall," the speaker will
inscribe death's "distinct grandiloquent/ deep D" and therein
find "perfection"[12] (*CP* 650), suffers from a lack of assurance;
the poem diffuses at its end, the central calligraphic image
modulating in death to something unclear—"and(plunging
rapturously up)/ we spill our masterpiece"—almost as if the
poet could not see far enough to make it whole. Only at the
close of his life did Cummings approach the lofty tone of late
Goethe or Yeats, facing the "deeper magic" (*CP* 675) of death
with a dignified but idiomatic simplicity, a distanced but in-
tensely personal vision, and a serene but passionate conviction
in transcendence.

   All this can be heard, I think, in the three lines of "wild(at
our first)," for the poem's two planes, a physical one of love-
making and a metaphysical one that moves through birth, love,
and death, balance and support married oppositions. On the
physical plane, Cummings uses a sexual pun he has used elsewhere—"lovers go and lovers come" (*CP* 591), a cliché slyly
rejuvenated—to create a love poem rich in overtones. Frost felt
that love, like poetry, "begins in delight and ends in wisdom,"[13]
and Cummings' luminous recounting of a night of it, passing
from the spoken ecstasies of first passion to still sweeter, un-
heard melodies, suggests full agreement. On the metaphysical
plane, "wild(at our first)" spans the compass of human existence, from the individuating cry of birth through the animating
song of love to the mysterious and transcendent silence of death.
It is here, beyond the physical, that the poem's harmonious progression—utterance, song, silence—finds richest implication.
Emerson, admiring the coherence of a primal realm, thought

"poetry was all written before time was,"[14] and Cummings embraces this idea in finding silence the most integrated music. In the world of flesh, "we lose ever and anon a word or a verse and substitute something of our own, and thus miswrite the poem";[15] beyond that world, however, in "the starhushed silence" of transcendence, we may fully grasp the poem, grow into perfect wholeness.

The perfect wholeness of "wild(at our first)" owes something to the natural correspondence of its planes, something to technical precision in the use of sound, echo, and syntax. Lovemaking, the poem's literal, earthy action, involves birth, death, and transcendence, and it functions therefore as a natural symbol of the poem's broader concerns; a generation, an expiration, and an ecstasy, it is at once a microcosm of existence and the fleshed being's best approximation of poetry "before time was." Technique in "wild(at our first)" intensifies the poem's movement. Love's initial passion and the shock of birth are suggested in the harsh *t*'s of the first line, while the dislocation of "wild . . . beasts," prolonging the adjective's suspension and creating double meaning (wild beasts, the usual phenomenon, and beasts driven wild), adds to the excitement. In the next line, alliteration and the voiced hum of *n*'s and *m*'s amplify the deeper harmony of singing stones, while the echo of a "second coming," far from flippant, concentrates the annunciated epochs of history into the interval of this triad's time. The last hushed line emphasizes its primacy of experience in the awed interjection "o" and the underlying echo of John Keats:

> Heard melodies are sweet, but those unheard
> Are sweeter; therefore, ye soft pipes, play on;
> Not to the sensual ear, but, more endear'd,
> Pipe to the spirit ditties of no tone.[16]

Like Keats's, Cummings' sensual sounds, born of craft and in a world of flesh, seek a farther range. And like Yeats's self-composed epitaph, this triad of Cummings'—the penultimate poem in his final book—at once summarizes his life and makes it noble.

5

FURNISHED SOULS

I have just been talking to a girl with a shrill monotonous voice and an abrupt way of moving. She is fresh from school, where they have taught her history and geography whereby 'a soul can be discerned,' but what is the value of an education, or . . . a science, that does not begin with the personality . . .?

—W. B. Yeats,
"Discoveries"

I am a government official & a goddamned fool.

—John Berryman,
The Dream Songs

"the Cambridge ladies who live in furnished souls" (CP 70)

the Cambridge ladies who live in furnished souls
are unbeautiful and have comfortable minds
(also, with the church's protestant blessings
daughters, unscented shapeless spirited)
they believe in Christ and Longfellow, both dead,
are invariably interested in so many things—
at the present writing one still finds
delighted fingers knitting for the is it Poles?
perhaps. While permanent faces coyly bandy
scandal of Mrs. N and Professor D
. . . . the Cambridge ladies do not care, above
Cambridge if sometimes in its box of
sky lavender and cornerless, the
moon rattles like a fragment of angry candy

Never given to faintness, Cummings damned as vigorously as he praised; his satire, mounting its attack from the self-assured ground of a firm moral superiority, thunders and flashes. Yet though its fierceness is Juvenalian, the satire is on the whole extraordinarily healthy. Devoid of the grotesque misogyny that sometimes marks this genre, never cynical, rarely rabid, Cummings' tirades are essentially the outbursts of a free and indignant spirit, unremarkably intolerant of a quite remarkable stupidity. Behind them we sense not the mannered smugness of the Age of Satire, but a saving naïveté, a humility of simple values. Introducing his miscalled *Collected Poems* (1938), the poet told his readers, "You and I are human beings;mostpeople are snobs"; yet he proceeded to justify fully this apparently snobbish remark:

> Mostpeople fancy a guaranteed birthproof safetysuit of nondestructible selflessness. If mostpeople were to be born twice they'd improbably call it dying—
> you and I are not snobs. We can never be born enough. We are human beings;for whom birth is a su-

premely welcome mystery,the mystery of growing: the
mystery which happens only and whenever we are
faithful to ourselves. You and I wear the dangerous
looseness of doom and find it becoming. (*CP* 461)

In the rich evocation of this last sentence we hear a celebrant
of all life, all mystery—no snob. In truth, the moral pedestal
upon which Cummings sets himself is the earth. If the dispen-
sation of his satire is liberal, this is because, amidst a teeming
populace of salesmen and "famous fatheads" (*CP* 411), cowards,
politicians, and "other punks" (*CP* 549), few human beings
seem to inhabit that planet.

Even the "uncommonwealth of humanusetts" (*CP* 325),
where Cabots, Lowells, God, and Harvard discriminately inter-
mingle, gives evidence of this paucity of life. To the west, at
Amherst, Emily Dickinson had noted it sixty years before—

> What Soft—Cherubic Creatures—
> These Gentlewomen are—
> One would as soon assault a Plush—
> Or violate a Star—[1]

and Cummings finds the same "Dimity Convictions—/ A Hor-
ror so refined/ Of freckled Human Nature—"[2] in "the Cambridge ladies who live in furnished souls." Thematically, this
sonnet requires little comment. Cummings' satire aims its ar-
rows at a broad, stationary target, the raft of faculty wives,
orchestral fund raisers, luncheon clubbers, church women, and
literary society ladies who comprise the socially prominent in
any academic community. Nor is the poet's critical angle, directed at the essential deadness of second-mind ideas rather than
first-hand feelings, oblique. What compels us is the way Cummings gives impact to his shots, the resonant twang of image
and the dead-center thump of exactly observed detail.

Accuracy begins with the poem's first lines. In the "furnished souls" and "comfortable minds" of the Cambridge ladies, Cummings wonderfully evokes the stuffy, proper Victorian
drawing rooms of their heads. Like "furnished rooms," the

phrase here echoed, these heads are both inflexibly set and set out by someone who does not live in them. Respectable above all, they display their standard, comfortable mental furniture, a thoughtlessly accepted morality of convention and a view of religion as social delineator. Not surprising, then, are the daughters of these heads: "unscented shapeless spirited," they collectively compose that repressed "Young Woman of cambridge, mass./ to whom nobody seems to have mentioned ye olde freudian wish" (*CP* 326).

The Cambridge ladies "believe in Christ and Longfellow" —a juxtaposition the more remarkable for the former's never having taught at Harvard—but only in the sense made swiftly apparent: "both dead." Activist Savior and benign poet are for them indistinguishably comfortable furnishings of culture. Christ's teaching of love—deflated into the mindless do-good-ism of "delighted fingers knitting for the is it Poles?"—is made as decorous, passionless, and ineffectual as Longfellow's poems.[3] Even the relative safety of vicarious experience cannot truly animate these women, whose faces remain "permanent" as they gossip. Like their Christ and Longfellow, the Cambridge la-dies are "dead"; straitened by artificiality, muffled in other people's ideas, they have learned to ward off the natural magic that surrounds them. Though the moon, object of natural piety and uncertain sphere of imagination,[4] "rattles like a fragment of angry candy," the Cambridge ladies "do not care."

Cummings generates satiric energy with other touches. Assuming at times the "spirited" voice of the ladies themselves, he derides by mimicry the cozy emptiness of their coffee-spoon lives: talking of Wadsworth Longfellow, they are "invariably interested in so many things," "at the present writing" delight-edly "knitting for the is it Poles?" In a related effect, the poet captures in sound the precious malice of these gossips, as they "coyly bandy/ scandal." Throughout, Cummings' language stresses the static, moribund quality of the women: by the time we have moved through "furnished souls," "comfortable minds," "both dead," and "invariably interested," "permanent faces" takes on the ring of epitaph.

Vividly contrasting the scattered vowels of these last formulations is the assonance of the moon, which "*rattles* like a fr*a*gment of *a*ngry c*a*ndy." And though it would be fanciful to suppose of another poet that the strange, symmetrical rhyme scheme here chosen, *abcddcba efggfe*, intends a graphic image—

a

b e

c f

d g

d g

c f

b e

a

—painter Cummings contrived such effects with a cheerful disregard for conventional poetic limits. The point is scarcely to be insisted upon. But what better way to evoke the synesthesia of a seen moon's angry rattle than to paint it in rhyme?

"proud of his scientific attitude" (CP 499)

proud of his scientific attitude

and liked the prince of wales wife wants to die
but the doctors won't let her comma considers frood
whom he pronounces young mistaken and
cradles in rubbery one somewhat hand
the paper destinies of nations sic
item a bounceless period unshy
the empty house is full O Yes of guk
rooms daughter item son a woopsing queer
colon hobby photography never has plumbed
the heights of prowst but respects artists if
they are sincere proud of his scientif
ic attitude and liked the king of)hear

ye!the godless are the dull and the dull are the damned

" 'The Kingdom of Heaven is no spiritual roofgarden: it's inside you,' " Cummings' father once announced to his parishioners;[5] and this very notion, the accessibility of human fulfillment, gave impetus to the poet's satire. Cummings fixed upon the perversion of adamic opportunity, upon the turning from active self-discovery or self-creation to deadening alternatives, precisely because self-creation is at once natural and necessary in his universe. Hate, the poet had learned from Dante, is but love perverted, and he applied this insight to the living dead around him. Their behavior came to seem not so much the result of a meaningful force, evil, as a willful disordering of natural good. And because it was willful, the result of mis-exercised freedom rather than social or psychological determinism, Cummings could feel a particular fury at the self-important perpetrators of this behavior. Thus, while he poured much of his energy into the celebration of lovers and growers —of Olaf and Joe Gould, "my father" and "my mother," Brave and Beautiful, noone and anyone[6]—he joyously exploded the remainder in blasts against the static, the stupid, the pompous, and the dull. Heroic "anyone" "sang his didn't [and] danced his did" (*CP* 515); like him, Cummings, damning and extolling with equal vigor, brought a creative exuberance to all his art.

This exuberance is audible in "proud of his scientific attitude," where an abundant energy spills sense across line ends, ignores the structural conventions of the traditional sonnet, and so heightens the effect of voice as to substantially mute metrical expectation. The poem's interweaving of cliché and vocal mimicry allies it to the improvisatory technique Cummings used in his infamous monologues—

> ". . . When without a word of warning what should happen but the whole hulk burst in flames and David Wark Griffith not standing by the shores of Gitcheegumme, by the shining big sea waters, where he used to paddle his own canoe, a birch bark canoe, guaranteed not to rust, leak or upset, children cry for it, women die for it . . ."[7]

—but a focusing of satiric attention and an underlying coherence of form generate poetic intensity. The result is a terse comedy of scorn. Aping the language of the poem's suitably nameless subject—a government official, we suspect—Cummings convicts him above all of his own words. The offense is crucial, for language expresses a way of conceiving the universe, and the man who speaks ill shows us that he lives badly.[8] Thus the platitudes, malapropisms, and general verbal palsy of the poem's subject are not harmlessly ridiculous; the murder of language suggests a corresponding spiritual destruction, and one which, beginning with the self, may reach out to destroy others. Not only dead, this poem's contemptible unhero is deadening as well.

Only the punctuation—where it is and where it isn't—and a few lines in the middle offer much difficulty. Where it is, spelled out, Cummings puns. Thus "comma" evokes "coma" and the condition of the subject's wife; "sic," not strictly punctuation, proclaims the demented circumstances that allow the poem's unhero to "cradle . . . in rubbery one somewhat hand/ the paper destinies of nations." "Period," in "a bounceless period unshy . . . daughter" (the intervening words, verbally parenthetic, are the narrator's ironic commentary), is ambiguous; part of an adjectival structure, it may suggest absoluteness or menstruation. "Bounceless, period!" might mean flat-chested, too tightly corseted, or simply dull; "bounceless period" would indicate a menstrual precision both mechanical and, obviously, infertile. "Colon" ("son a whoopsing queer/ colon") is where homosexual love pitches its mansion.

The absence of other punctuation suggests the run-on, undifferentiated nature of the people described: subject, wife, son, and daughter are all, as the son's "inhuman/ itarian fetish" (*CP* 492) demonstrates, essentially interchangeable, because all refuse the natural roles that would define their individualities. Child-giving wife does not want to live, daughter is unfeminine, son unmasculine. The patriarch of this damned family, instead of fostering individual growth, worships any authority ("liked the prince of wales," "liked the king of"); instead of loving well, he thinks badly. Cummings lampoons him—perhaps "harpoons" would be the more accurate verb—with mispronunciation ("considers frood [Freud]/ whom he pronounces young [Jung: a pun as well on "wrong"] mistaken"), with the substitution of cliché for thought ("respects artists if/ they are sincere"), and with the triumphant confusion of it all: "never has plumbed/ the heights of prowst." Even grammatical structure enforces the essential nonexistence of this unhero; though "he" is the understood subject of half the sonnet's fourteen verbs—"liked," "considers," "pronounces," "cradles," "has plumbed," "respects," and again "liked"—only once, and in a dependent clause, does the nominative pronoun appear. In grammar as in spirit, this poem's subject lacks identity.

Cummings' forceful tirade turns neatly at the close to a moral, rounding and expanding his sonnet sermon. The single close parenthesis puts everything before it into subordinate focus, as if the narrator, like Vergil guiding Dante through *Inferno*, had turned away from some damned soul to make a final, monitory comment. As with so many of the souls in *Inferno*, we have seen this poem's subject in a futile, repetitious cycle, coming into verbal sight with a tag—"proud of his scientific attitude/ and liked the prince of wales"—and disappearing —"proud of his scientif/ ic attitude and liked the king of"— just as a similar tag is repeated. The concluding comment, too, has the severe and formal ring of Dante's guide. Its "hear ye!" may contain an ironic thrust at the subject's admiration for authority, "prince" and "king," but it is primarily a lofty demand for attention. And though the final apothegm embodies a typically Cummingsean reversal—the godless are conventionally last accused of dullness, the dull last thought likely to be damned—its meaning is clear. The "godless" are those hubristic reasoners who would attempt to explain away the mysteries of nature. They are the objectifiers, men of that "fundamentally . . . depersonalizing leveler" (*L* 265), science. Not individuals, they are "dull." And doomed to exist in a loveless vacuum—for only individuals can love—they are "damned" as well. These hollow men pursue the empty, mechanical circle "round the prickly pear"; they end "Not with a bang but a whimper," or, like Swift's terrible Struldbruggs and the present poem's comatose wife, they do not end at all.[9]

"MEMORABILIA" (CP 256)

stop look &

listen Venezia: incline thine
ear you glassworks
of Murano;
pause
elevator nel
mezzo del cammin' that means half-
way up the Campanile, believe

thou me cocodrillo—

mine eyes have seen
the glory of

the coming of
the Americans particularly the
brand of marriageable nymph which is
armed with large legs rancid
voices Baedekers Mothers and kodaks
—by night upon the Riva Schiavoni or in
the felicitous vicinity of the de l'Europe

Grand and Royal
Danielli their numbers

are like unto the stars of Heaven. . . .

i do signore
affirm that all gondola signore
day below me gondola signore gondola
and above me pass loudly and gondola

Furnished Souls
81

rapidly denizens of Omaha Altoona or what
not enthusiastic cohorts from Duluth God only,
gondola knows Cincingondolanati i gondola don't

—the substantial dollarbringing virgins

"from the Loggia where
are we angels by O yes
beautiful we now pass through the look
girls in the style of that's the
foliage what is it didn't Ruskin
says about you got the haven't Marjorie
isn't this wellcurb simply darling"
                                   —O Education:O

thos cook & son

(O to be a metope
now that triglyph's here)

    Yeats's words that serve as epigraph to this chapter—they
are from his essay "Discoveries"—suggest the basis of Cummings' satire in "MEMORABILIA." "What," the Irishman had
asked rhetorically, "is the value of an education . . . that does
not begin with the personality?" Cummings' poem, portrait of
a Venice fragmented, illuminates this lament. The tourists
here painted have become acquirers rather than creators, for
their education began not with the personality but with that
external to it. They have learned to purchase, photograph, and
catalogue ideas and objects, but they connect nothing of art and
culture with themselves. Failing to sense the inherent contra-
diction between absorbing the stones of Venice and discussing
them in "rancid voices," they destroy the very culture they
stalk. On a trip to Venice made the same year as "MEMORA-
BILIA," Cummings saw the "intrinsically wrong . . . sign
'SOMETHING NEW, CHEAP AND BEAUTIFUL'" and
observed sadly that this "glittering slogan . . . reflects, all too
well, our own nation's slip-shod method of thought."[10] Money
changers, in short—either acquisitive tourists or the predatory

hawkers that spring up around them—profane art's temples as well as God's. And where, as in Venice, the two are one, a whole city may grow gaunt amidst the din.

A title, always noteworthy when it occurs in Cummings' work, sets the tone of this poem. Echoing Robert Browning, who died in Venice and whose lines will be modified for the poem's close, it gathers at once both loss and irony. Browning's "Memorabilia" fixes on the remembered moment, the image that remains when its context has vanished:

> I crossed a moor, with a name of its own
> And a certain use in the world no doubt,
> Yet a hand's-breadth of it shines alone
> 'Mid the blank miles round about:
>
> For there I picked upon the heather
> And there I put inside my breast
> A moulted feather, an eagle-feather!
> Well, I forget the rest.[11]

Cummings' Venetian eagle-feather, the image that remains after splendors of history, art, and architecture are forgotten, is this dramatic vocal impression of a city fragmented. In its idiomatic mixture of Browning, railroad talk, Dante, Julia Ward Howe, and the King James Bible, in its contrapuntal treatment of poetic speaker and omnipresent gondolier, and above all in its vocal cacophony of female tourists, the poems recreates a modern Babel.

Yet Venice once ruled the seas. From this city Marco Polo had begun his famous journeys; to it Dante had been sent as ambassador by Guido da Polenta. As late as 1911 Mann's Gustav Aschenbach could think: "Wenn man über Nacht das Unvergleichliche, das märchenhaft Abweichende zu erreichen wünschte, wohin ging man? Aber das war klar."[12] Fifteen years later, though—to a perhaps less tolerant observer—the city was virtually dead, its mysterious balance of East and West overwhelmed by the influx of Americanism. Cummings quotes a gondolier—"Venice,city of silence & poetry,is murdered by

Furnished Souls
83

motorboats" (*L* 248)[13]—and leaves, at and in the city's wake, this memorabilia.

The precision here is difficult to set down, but it resides in ironies. Once a center of culture, sea power Venice has become accessible primarily by train, has devolved into a mere railroad crossing. Once a home of learned men, Venice is now visited by mistranslation, Dante's "nel mezzo del cammin' "—"in the middle of the journey," the allegorical beginning of the *Divina Commedia*—here misrendered "half-/ way up the Campanile," the tower before St. Mark's cathedral. These invaders are not God's forces, the grim waves of Civil War soldiers in Miss Howe's "Battle Hymn of the Republic," but money's, "the substantial dollarbringing virgins." And though Cummings' description of them involves comedies of pun and especially sound —"armed with . . . legs," "Baedekers Mothers and kodaks," "in/ the felicitous vicinity"—his poem tramples out the vintage of wrath's grapes.

The opening, long sentence of "Memorabilia" establishes the poem's theme and tonality; the remainder consists of two variations on that theme and a coda. First is the almost operatic counterpoint of harassed speaker and persistent gondolier, an uncomfortable duet whose occurrence the speaker blames on money. As the duet develops, sense, straightforward, becomes less important than sound; "gondola" (its accent is on the initial syllable) merges with "Omaha" and "Altoona," and the passage moves toward a comically ridiculous fusion of the United States and Italy. It reaches this in "Cincingondolanati," the unmusical affadavit that buyer and seller are indissolubly and ruinously interdependent. There follows a cinematic passage, rapid cuts jarring against one another until, regardless of conventional content, technique itself makes statement. Within the quotation marks I hear fourteen different (or alternating) voices—all at cross purposes, none identifiable—and the effect of their running together is a dramatic aural metaphor. "Only connect," E. M. Forster prefaced *Howards End*, and we see here the consequences of ignoring him. Amidst the decaying but still appreciable splendors of Venice, John Ruskin and anonymous Marjorie have nothing to say to each other. Faced with magnificent buildings and paintings, the disconnected tourist can feel only with her second-head sensibility, speak only in her trivializing idiom; beneath the awesome shadow of *San Marco*, she asks: "isn't this wellcurb simply darling."

The poem's coda, superb in its crescendo of O's, gathers final scorn. Its juxtaposition of "Education" and "thos cook & son" (purveyors of Cook's tours and once the cheapest traveler's checks) suggests the unholy alliance between knowledge and money that has led to the desecration of Venice and the ruin of her destroyers. The final lines, harkening back to an echo in the title, alter Browning's "Home-Thoughts, from Abroad." "Oh to be in England/ Now that April's there," the homesick Englishman had written,[14] but Cummings, longing for a change of atmosphere rather than place, wishes only to be free of the cacophony that precedes this coda. In "O to be a metope/ now that triglyph's here," he replaces Browning's poignance with comedy—the chime of "be" and "metope" is as responsible for this difference as the shift in language—and offers an ironic summary of his feelings. Desiring to be a metope, the space in a Doric frieze between projecting, ornamental triglyphs, Cummings would disappear from the loud and aggressive young women of his land. Casting a last, parenthesized Venetian stone, the poet exits with a stage whisper, trailing his dismay at the "marriageable nymph" abroad.

"here is little Effie's head" (CP 117)

here is little Effie's head
whose brains are made of gingerbread
when the judgment day comes
God will find six crumbs

stooping by the coffinlid
waiting for something to rise

Furnished Souls
85

as the other somethings did—
you imagine His surprise

bellowing through the general noise
Where is Effie who was dead?
—to God in a tiny voice,
i am may the first crumb said

whereupon its fellow five
crumbs chuckled as if they were alive
and number two took up the song,
might i'm called and did no wrong

cried the third crumb, i am should
and this is my little sister could
with our big brother who is would
don't punish us for we were good;

and the last crumb with some shame
whispered unto God, my name
is must and with the others i've
been Effie who isn't alive

just imagine it I say
God amid a monstrous din
watch your step and follow me
stooping by Effie's little, in

(want a match or can you see?)
which the six subjunctive crumbs
twitch like mutilated thumbs:
picture His peering biggest whey

coloured face on which a frown
puzzles, but I know the way—
(nervously Whose eyes approve
the blessed while His ears are crammed

with the strenuous music of
the innumerable capering damned)
—staring wildly up and down
the here we are now judgment day

cross the threshold have no dread
lift the sheet back in this way.
here is little Effie's head
whose brains are made of gingerbread

Modern poets, like modern writers in general, have had little to say for organized religion. Across the Atlantic, Eliot, who struggled to a final orthodoxy, was more than counterpoised by Yeats and Dylan Thomas, who rejected the passivity they found in Christian doctrine. On this side—I have left Eliot where he settled and grew native—only Auden and Robert Lowell come to mind as major religious poets in the narrow sense, and the English transplant returned to Europe before his death. Meanwhile Stevens, Frost, Roethke, Cummings, Dickey, and most of our other important poets have taken directions tangential to the circle of orthodoxy. Cummings' position, typically romantic, is short on doctrine, long on metaphor. For him, God is the illimitable mystery behind motion, love, and process, the "unimaginable You" that no "human merely being/ [can] doubt" (*CP* 663); broad enough to embrace all action, Cummings' God encompasses at once Thomas' "force that through the green fuse drives the flower" and Dante's "L' amor che move il sole e l' altre stelle" (the love that moves the sun and all the stars).[15] However expansive his conception of deity, though, Cummings is satirically definitive about what God is not. In "here is little Effie's head," he routs not only the frightened little soul of his protagonist, but the presumed theology behind it; with his portrait of a confused and ineffectual deity, Cummings debunks the idea of a prohibitive and retributive God, certified cosmic accountant of meeknesses.

Little Effie is the supremely passive soul, shrinking timidly through a brittle, china-shop life. The "may," "might," "should," "could," "would," and "must" that comprise her brain, the six subjunctive gingerbread crumbs, mark only a shadow world, a place not of real happenings but of the conditional existence that was for Cummings nonexistence. The poet would of course have agreed with Emily Dickinson's visionary credo, "I dwell in Possibility—/ A fairer House than Prose,"[16] but only because that possibility was active and imaginative. Toward limiting injunctions—and we may note here that nine of the ten commandments forbid—Cummings had only scorn. "An artist, a man, a failure, MUST PROCEED," says a character in one of the poet's plays,[17] and Effie, shirking this universal responsibility to act, in effect ceases to live; she has done "no wrong," but, being "good" by being no one, she has relinquished her humanness. As Thomas would bitterly chastise those passive wartime Christians who "could not stir/ One lean sigh when we heard/ Greed on man beating near and fire neighbour/ But wailed and nested in the sky-blue wall,"[18] as John Berryman would sicken at a President elected "to a second term, having done no wrong—/ no right—no right,"[19] so Cummings before them denigrates "Effie who isn't alive"—and wasn't.[20]

At stake, however, is something more than a single wasted life. Transforming the awesome atmosphere of Judgment Day into the busy commotion of a carnival, Cummings undermines the theological props supporting his protagonist. Instead of the solemn admitting angels with their clarion horns, he records the noisy spiel of shills ("watch your step and follow me," "cross the threshold have no dread," "lift the sheet back in this way"); instead of the usual God of wrath, poised and terrible, he offers a puzzled, whey-faced carny. Cummings' point is clear: a God who elects the blessed for their failure to act rather than the passion of their actions suppresses the very root of life. Such a God negates the essence of what He has made, contradicts Himself. In the poem, as His eyes

> (nervously . . . approve
> the blessed while His ears are crammed
>
> with the strenuous music of
> the innumerable capering damned),

God becomes a Maker superannuated by His own creation, a

Father whose values are less joyful and less true than the values of His children.

Meter is the technical key to "little Effie." The simple and regular four-beat line generates a childlike lightness, an easy and unsolemn mood appropriate to this amusing moral parable. At the same time, such regularity sets us up for its important contravention. Everything here—Effie, the subjunctive crumbs that speak for her, even God—is too static, too limited, and we appreciate this finally through meter. We may be initially perplexed at Cummings' carnival of Judgment, but the celebrative vitality of those "capering damned" and their "strenuous music" lead us to suspect a theological reversal. Meter confirms it. Once we see "good"ness marching to a regular metrical beat—

        x ∪ x   ∪ x ∪ x
    (nervously Whose eyes approve
        ∪ x ∪ (x) ∪ x   x
    the blessed while His ears are crammed—

once we hear the freer drummer associated

      ∪   ∪ x ∪∪   x∪ ∪
    with the strenuous music of
    ∪ ∪ x ∪∪∪ x ∪∪   x
    the innumerable capering damned),

we can be certain that this God's favorites are not Cummings', and *vice versa*. Amidst gingerbrained Effie, whey-faced God, and the anonymous blessed, only the "capering damned" here have the poet's admiration. It is they who are truly blessed, for, ignoring the blandness of conditional existence, they have embraced the "strenuous music" of living.

"everybody happy?" (CP 791)

    everybody happy?
    WE-WE-WE
    & to hell with the chappy
    who doesn't agree

(if you can't dentham
comma bentham;
or 1 law for the lions &
oxen is science)

Q:how numb can an unworld get?
A:number

Satire is at bottom an epigrammatic talent, and while
Cummings could excel in such expansive pieces as "Poem, or
Beauty Hurts Mr. Vinal" (*CP* 230) and "MEMORABILIA"
(*CP* 256), perhaps his best work in this genre is his briefest.
No one can read the devastating quatrain on Hemingway—

what does little Ernest croon
in his death at afternoon?
(kow dow r 2 bul retoinis
wus de woids uf lil Oinis (*CP* 409)

—without looking just a bit less seriously at the novelist's celebrated toughness; no one who sees

a politician is an arse upon
which everyone has sat except a man (*CP* 550)

can nod quite as easily at political compromise. But Cummings
brought great satiric compression to broader subjects as well.
In "everybody happy?" he spans the century and three quarters
between William Blake and the present in order to attack the
depersonalizing forces alternative to individuality. Punning
with sight and sound, gaining economy, authority, and humor
from allusion, he strikes in ten short lines a decisive blow for
uniqueness.

"Is *ev*-erybody *hap*-py?" top-hatted Ted Lewis used to ask
—his trademark—and the vaudeville audiences would respond
with a chorused "yeah!" Creating satiric tension, Cummings'
version of this exchange combines the French "*oui*," the English first person plural pronoun, and the last little piggy's cry
("wee wee wee all the way home"). The target here is stand-
ardization, "to hell with the chappy/ who doesn't agree," and

Cummings' barbed shafts find the bull's-eye. Neither strategy —the old saw, "if you can't lick them, join them," echoes behind sight rhymed "dentham"—nor political and ethical theory —Jeremy Bentham's utilitarianism claimed that the greatest happiness of the greatest number was the proper measure of right and wrong[21]—could alter the sacredness of the individual, and Cummings' scorn for anything less is neatly condensed: "(if you can't dentham/ comma bentham." When we remember that Carlyle spoke of Bentham's doctrine as "pig philosophy," the second line's full measure of satire becomes apparent.

In "1 law for the lions &/ oxen is science," we have an updated rendering of *The Marriage of Heaven and Hell*. "One Law for the Lion & Ox is Oppression," the individualistic Blake had written,[22] and with his revision Cummings thrusts this credo firmly into the twentieth century. Science, that "depersonalizing leveller" (*L* 265), substitutes quantity for quality, number for nature; but "for me nothing impersonal or measureable matters," the poet wrote Eva Hesse, while "for science measureability and impersonality are everything" (*L* 265). Bentham had minutely quantified the value of pains and pleasures, and it is to the Benthams of his own age that Cummings addresses his final lines:

Q:how numb can an unworld get?
A:number.

There is a splendid finality to this concluding pun. Its coincidence of comparative adjective and mathematical noun seems almost a reflection of Platonic reality, as if it must somehow be the same in all languages. And though of course it is not, this sense establishes with emotional certainty the poet's central claim. Qualitative experience, essentially mysterious, is the stuff of living; its abolition transforms a sentient universe to numb unworld.

6

LOVE'S FUNCTION

*And I dance with William Blake
For love, for Love's sake;*

*And everything comes to One,
As we dance on, dance on, dance on.*

—Theodore Roethke
"Once More, the Round"

"one's not half two. It's two are halves of one:" (CP 556)

one's not half two. It's two are halves of one:
which halves reintegrating,shall occur
no death and any quantity;but than
all numerable mosts the actual more

minds ignorant of stern miraculous
this every truth—beware of heartless them
(given the scalpel,they dissect a kiss;
or,sold the reason,they undream a dream)

one is the song which fiends and angels sing:
all murdering lies by mortals told make two.
Let liars wilt,repaying life they're loaned;
we(by a gift called dying born)must grow

deep in dark least ourselves remembering
love only rides his year.
All lose,whole find

    In the emotional topography of Cummings' world there stands beyond the pleasant country of seduction a deeper, more mysterious realm, the transcendent place of fully realized love. Here the ceremonious banter of him and her is relinquished, the ardent and arduous strategies of proposition dropped. Instead, the poetic speaker assumes a seriousness reserved for the most sacred occasions. As Cummings develops the metaphysics of this realm—through a series of paradoxes nearly homomorphic to the Christian ones—he reveals the strongly classical bent of his romanticism. Indeed, wide as is the gap of time between ancient Greek and modern American poet, there stretches only a distance of metaphor between that stern tenet of Aeschylus, "$\Delta\acute{\iota}\chi\alpha$ $\delta\acute{\epsilon}$ $\tau o\iota\varsigma$ $\mu\acute{\epsilon}\nu$ $\pi\alpha\theta o\upsilon\sigma\iota/$ $\mu\alpha\theta\epsilon\iota\nu$ $\acute{\epsilon}\pi\acute{\iota}\phi\phi\acute{\epsilon}\pi\epsilon\iota$" ("Justice allots wisdom to those who suffer"),[1] and Cummings' own rigorous credo, "we(by a gift called dying born)must grow"; to realize lofty gaiety, both poets tell us, we must pass gladly through worlds of innocence and experience, paying freely the price of each.

For Cummings, love is both the means to and the end of this transcendence. Its interpenetrating demands move us to the physical death of orgasm and the spiritual one of loss, but both kinds of dying lead to birth. This is the poet's dialectic of growth: life—aliveness rather than mere existence—is a constant process of becoming by surrendering; to love is to embrace that process. Yet the dynamic soul, born over and over, moves always toward a higher, more integral reality, and may ultimately achieve a coherence, a miraculous wholeness, at once dynamic and absolute. Love, the means, will then have reached the Dantean beatitude of love, the end.

Such explanation, of course, does violence at every turn of phrase to the delicacy of Cummings' conception; generalizing —divorcing significance from the poetic process of its happening—it bespeaks murderous dissection. And this is the very lesson of "one's not half of two. It's two are halves of one." This holy sonnet, sharing with Donne and Dylan Thomas a metaphysical imagination that delights in paradox and the serious use of sexual imagery, reaches beyond its literal, cavalier situation from the very start. There is of course a seductive suggestion to the first line, but the emphatic weight of its initial spondees—

$$\overset{\times}{\text{one's}}\ \overset{\times}{\text{not}}\ \overset{\times}{\text{half}}\ \overset{\times}{\text{two}}$$

—particularly as they underline paradox, points to a larger significance. An echo of Plato sustains this impression. The phrase "halves reintegrating" may extend the mathematical language of line 1, but as it catches Aristophanes' voice in the *Symposium*, it brings to his limited parable of sexuality that dialogue's broader concern for the whole of love. "One," then, the word beginning both octave and sestet, is this sonnet's chief concern, and the unity Cummings evokes is not merely of lovers but of love's antinomies. On a literal level, the poem moves toward sexual union, its speaker persuades his lady; the metaphoric thrust is toward a marriage of flesh and spirit, ἔρος and ἀγάπη. Achieved, these movements outstrip the realm of particular quantity, however large; they enable the lover to rise above "numerable mosts," limited and dead, to reach "the actual more," boundless, alive, and therefore real. As with Donne's God—in "death, thou shalt die"[2]—and Thomas' organicism— in "And death shall have no dominion"[3]—Cummings' love defeats time and space; in its fulfillment occurs "no death and any quantity."

A strong emotional self-discipline, however, is required for this fulfillment. Mind, Cummings' Satan, tempts us either to ratiocinative cowardice or to intellectual pride; either we pause to calculate, and the moment in the rose garden vanishes, or we calculate proudly how we do not pause. Keeper of self-consciousness, mediator between impulse and deed, mind weighs too heavily the shadows of the world without; it sees differences, not unity; it divides. So doing, it falsifies the transcendent reality that is for Cummings the *only* reality. In the implicative verbal contrast of this sonnet's third quatrain, feelings "sing," embrace the wholeness of truth; mind, however, tells—the word connotes mathematical tally as well as flat narration—; it lies. This explains the poet's antirationalism, a romantic tradition to whose service Cummings calls, by the juxtaposition of "dissect" and "murdering," the spirit of William Wordsworth. Because love alone can perceive the wholeness of phenomena, and because only through such perception can a man truly live, "The Tables Turned" makes here a forceful background; in Cummings' world, we quite literally "murder to dissect."[4] Liars transact without interest the business of existence and "wilt,repaying life they're loaned"; given a talent they bury it securely. Singers, though—lovers—risking everything on the joy of surrender, increase their store; they "(by a gift called dying born)must grow."

Cummings' final lines articulate the discipline requisite to such increase. Seedlike lovers "must grow/ deep in dark"— they must become adepts in the service of essential mystery— "least [themselves] remembering," by surrender to another rather than egotistic self-importance. At the same time (Cummings' double syntax, two things in one, creates and resolves the paradox), they must "grow/ deep"—develop fullness of character—"in dark[,] least [themselves]," for without a humble embrace of the limited self, limitless surrender is impossible. Nor may love's servants tarry: "love only rides his year." Like Isaac McCaslin abandoning watch and compass,[5] or Frost's guided traveler, the lover must become "lost enough to find [him]self."[6] When he has done so, the Bear, the transcendent vision, will be manifest. "All lose,whole find."

The four stark accents of this last sentence—

$$\overset{x}{\text{All}} \ \overset{x}{\text{lose,}}\overset{x}{\text{whole}} \ \overset{x}{\text{find}}$$

—are a concluding technical stroke of rich precision. Underscoring the summary paradox of the poem, they echo as well the speaker's serious attitude toward it. Indeed, their very weight consolidates the thematic point that sense, structure, and diction have moved toward. In the rigors of the sonnet form, particularly the unique, symmetrical double spondees that begin and end this sonnet, aesthetic discipline creates a sense of unity. Through a vocabulary that bounds romantic vagueness ("miraculous," "deep") with hard edges ("stern," "reintegrate"), the poem expresses the stringent requisites of transcendent love.

"anyone lived in a pretty how town" (CP 515)

anyone lived in a pretty how town
(with up so floating many bells down)
spring summer autumn winter
he sang his didn't he danced his did.

Women and men(both little and small)
cared for anyone not at all
they sowed their isn't they reaped their same
sun moon stars rain

children guessed(but only a few
and down they forgot as up they grew
autumn winter spring summer)
that noone loved him more by more

when by now and tree by leaf
she laughed his joy she cried his grief
bird by snow and stir by still
anyone's any was all to her

someones married their everyones
laughed their cryings and did their dance
(sleep wake hope and then)they
said their nevers they slept their dream

stars rain sun moon
(and only the snow can begin to explain
how children are apt to forget to remember
with up so floating many bells down)

one day anyone died i guess
(and noone stooped to kiss his face)
busy folk buried them side by side
little by little and was by was

all by all and deep by deep
and more by more they dream their sleep
noone and anyone earth by april
wish by spirit and if by yes.

Women and men(both dong and ding)
summer autumn winter spring
reaped their sowing and went their came
sun moon stars rain

Cummings' poetic speakers have often specific and highly vocal opinions; the instinct to preach, perhaps an inheritance from the poet's father, Reverend Edward Cummings, is never long suppressed. Sometimes, though, the action of a poem is commentary enough, and only in his choice of the words to convey it does the poet show where his heart lies. Such is the case with the remarkable, much anthologized "anyone lived in a pretty how town." Taking shape largely through the characterizing force of verbal contrasts, this childlike yet sophisticated narrative pleases nearly everyone. And well it might. Out of his talent for stirring words to lively pattern, Cummings has fashioned both a moving testimony to the power of love and a portrait of lovelessness that indicts itself.

Contrast is key here, between celebration and empty ritual, love and lip service, life and death-in-life. The poem tells of "anyone" and "noone," pronominal hero and heroine, whose love for life and each other creates a rich and finally transcendent togetherness. Failing in the weight of truth to counterpoise them, but serving as structural foils, are "Women and men," "someones and everyones"—the mass of nonbeings leading their lives of fatuously self-important desperation. Children, hope of the future, fill out the *dramatis personae*, but as they move toward "maturity, . . . that eternal process/ Most obsessively wrong with the world,"[7] they literally forget themselves; natural piety recedes, emotional growth varies inversely with chronological. Ultimately "anyone" and "noone," having lived, may die; the town's remaining, static inhabitants continue a prickly-pear existence, endlessly rounding the dull hell they have made of their world.

The first stanza introduces most of the technical devices of this graceful, fluid poem. With the use of the pronominal name, "anyone," Cummings economically accomplishes three things: he is able to suggest the accessibility of emotional liveliness (anybody willing to make the sacrifices can be "anyone"), he can imply the townspeople's lack of regard for our hero (nothing special, he is just "anyone" to them), and he can prepare the unique double usage ("anyone" as both name and ordinary pronoun) that makes possible the poem's simultaneous specificity and breadth. With "a pretty how town," Cummings inverts a cliché and breathes new life into its elements; he transforms the usual scrubbed shrubberies and ordered lawns—"how pretty a town!"—into ominous echo; for

"how" is here adjectival, a "how town" one where the particular way of doing things rather than the feeling behind them
matters most. The syntactic dislocations of line 2 are another
fine stroke. Through their rhythmic juxtaposition of "floating"
and "bells," "up" and "down," Cummings evokes the musical
pendulum of church bells, and, in the sensual apprehension of
their meaning—day and night, peace and war, birth and death
—extends this music to suggest the passing of time itself. Line
3 intensifies the effect as it limns the cycle of natural growth.
Almost metronomic, its four beats—musically,

spring summer autumn winter

—mark time both for the poem and for its world.[8] The stanza's
final line, making vivid nominative use of "didn't" and "did,"
demonstrates the poet's ability to raise "abstractions . . . to the
power of the concrete."[9] At the same time, its verbs define and
intensify the statement of line 1: singing and dancing, whether
of "didn't" or "did," "anyone" is an incorrigible celebrant, active and joyous. As the whole poem makes clear, his emotional
affirmation is the root meaning of "lived."

Negation, in contrast, is the way of "Women and men."
Not big and small, the ordinary physical assortment, they are
"little and small," unvaried and emotionally stunted; cool to
the poem's hero, they love nobody else either. Having learned
nothing from Galatians 6:7—"whatsoever a man soweth, that
shall he also reap"—these townspeople waste their lives and
recycle their lovelessness; in time—"they sowed their isn't they
reaped their same/ sun moon stars rain"—a similar emptiness
descends upon their children. For though some "children
guessed"—the uncertain verb suggests intuitive feeling—that a
girl named "noone" loved the poem's hero, their awareness
fades before the emotional stupor around them; in the face of
the pronominal fact that no one loves anyone, these children
forget the nominative truth, "noone" loves "anyone."

Yet that truth is the poem's center. "Noone"'s love, at

once a sharing of feeling and an intensification of it—"she laughed his joy she cried his grief"—fills the space in "anyone"'s open heart. As a bird brings the quickening of spring to snowy winter or an autumn breeze sharpens summer's stillness—"bird by snow and stir by still"—she brings liveliness to her lover; townspeople "cared for anyone not at all," but "anyone's any was all to her." Dead to life, on the other hand, "someones" and "everyones" substitute marriage, "public promises/ of one's intention/ to fullfill a private obligation,"[10] for love. Cummings cleverly underlines the perversion of their values with a turning of his own. Whereas "anyone" "danced his did" and "noone" "laughed [anyone's] joy," the townspeople "laughed their cryings and did their dance." Lacking the courage for intensity, they cultivate blandness; lacking the creative impulse of celebration, they can follow only empty ritual. Instead of prayers, they say "nevers."

And so passes the cycle of life. Eventually "anyone" and "noone" die—together, as they have lived—and are hastily interred by still self-important "busy folk." Yet even in death they "dream their sleep," an active formulation that suggests transcendence, whereas the physically alive townspeople have throughout "slept their dream." Death is but a continuation of growth for this poem's loving pair, but its "Women and men" remain perennially dead. "Anyone" and "noone" move past the townspeople's slight and slighting epitaph, "little by little and was by was," to fulfill the narrator's rich tribute, "wish by spirit and if by yes." Their treadmill antagonists slog endlessly on.

Nowhere is Cummings more lyrically inventive. With a sudden present tense after we have grown accustomed to the narrative past—"dream their sleep"—he can generate metaphysical propositions a philosopher (or explicator) would need lines to expound. Perhaps we must read Dante—"cotal son io, chè quasi tutta cessa/ Mia visione . . . ./ Così la neve al sol si disigilla." (So it is with me: The vision that was mine/ Has almost wholly faded . . . ./ Thus the snow unseals itself in sunshine.")[11] —fully to understand how "only the snow can begin to explain/ how children are apt to forget to remember," but the wistful lilt alone of these lines creates much of their sense. Even so slight a phrase as the final stanza's "dong and ding" resonates richly; combining an echo of the poem's floating bells with a recollection of the earlier parallel image, "little and small" (nothing to choose between), it harvests structural, musical, and even visual seeds. For Cummings, "Women and men" must always be first individuals; with "dong and ding" he implies their refusal to be so. Identifying these groups at the simplest, slang level of their difference, feminine "dong" and masculine "ding," he makes us aware of how similar they sound. His fine phrase suggests that but for the visual representation of their sexualities—the *o* of "dong," the *i* of "ding" —these townspeople are identical copies of each other, sheep stapled and folded.

"love's function is to fabricate unknownness" (CP 446)

love's function is to fabricate unknownness

(known being wishless;but love,all of wishing)
though life's lived wrongsideout,sameness chokes oneness
truth is confused with fact,fish boast of fishing

and men are caught by worms(love may not care
if time totters,light droops,all measures bend
nor marvel if a thought should weigh a star
—dreads dying least;and less,that death should end)

how lucky lovers are(whose selves abide
under whatever shall discovered be)
whose ignorant each breathing dares to hide
more than most fabulous wisdom fears to see

(who laugh and cry)who dream,create and kill
while the whole moves;and every part stands still:

Cummings saw our century quantify nearly everything, illumine even creatures of the deep in the flat, shadowless glare of reason and research; and he writhed, like Grendel in the grip of Beowulf, to keep some darkness in our world. This is of course not to align him with the descendants of Cain, but to suggest his mortal struggle against an intellectual climate that robs modern man of privacy, uniqueness, and therefore freedom. Like Dostoyevski's underground man, Cummings embraced the absolute freedom of his desires, particularly where they conflicted with the builders of crystal palaces, where they rejected the deterministic meliorism of modern social science; *tout comprendre c'est tout pardonner*—the century's enlightened amorality—he held to be an insultingly limited view of human existence. Instead, siding with Roethke—"We think by feeling. What is there to know?"[12]—he found life too much a miracle to explain.

In "love's function is to fabricate unknownness," Cummings tries to evoke a sense of that miracle. "Joy," he would later say, "[is] a mystery at right angles equally to pain & pleasure, as truth is to fact & fiction";[13] and love's function is to move the lover toward this mysterious, transcendent reality. It must do so over the pressing claims of the mundane, for in the dreamless unworld of "mostpeople" (*CP* 461), "life's lived wrongsideout," rational, practical, and egotistic considerations stifle the spirit; to cite Roethke again, "the rind, often, hates the life within."[14] In the unworld, conformity and routine clog the path to transcendence, the metaphysical and mundane are jumbled; "sameness chokes oneness/ truth is confused with fact. Inversion turns toward self-destruction—"fish boast of fishing"—and means, subverting ends, assume control of their devisers, "men are caught by worms."

Antidotal to this inversion of values is love. Absolute in itself, love is beyond the reach of exterior causality; a fixed point amidst the dislocations of Einsteinian relativity, it brushes aside mere physical cataclysm, "may not care/ if time totters,light droops,all measures bend." Fearing nothing, it welcomes both death and transcendence, "dreads dying least;and less,that death should end." Love is the essential mystery, the irreducible spiritual atom, and its embracers, creating always new and unfathomable privacies, are as far beyond the scope of wisdom as intuition is beyond probability theory. Active lovers, "who laugh and cry . . . dream,create and kill," experience the paradoxical, paradisiacal beatitude of Dante. As "the whole moves;and every part stands still," an embellishment of the *Paradiso* and of "Burnt Norton," they sing love's synergy.[15] For "the whole moves" suggests not only kinesis but feeling, and "every part stands still" conveys longevity as well as fixity. The paradox of movement, then, resolves itself through emotion: stirred—moved—by a sense of wholeness, of unity, lovers transcend time.

The poem's craft helps us feel rather than understand all this, however philosophical its subject. Enlivening by contrast, Cummings particularizes abstractions—"unknownness," "sameness," "oneness," "truth," "fact"—and thereby eliminates the need to define terms or state assumptions. He asks that we respond not scientifically but aesthetically, not to logic but to the resonance of words; and if we do, the connotative overtones of language pipe rich harmonics. "Fishing," for example, combines its usual, specific sense, an angler's pastime, with the vaguer, more general one, to hopefully grope; and thus the confusion of "fish boast of fishing" grows in meaning to include the muddling of limited, quantitative experience—*this* big—with uncertain and lively action. "Worms," not merely fish bait but agent of decomposition, expands similarly: imaging death as well as inversion, "men are caught by worms" comes to imply both the subversion of means to ends and the result of it, the soulless finality of death in the unworld. Even form contributes to thematic vividness. "Love's function" concerns the making of private wholes, synergistic unities, and the formal coherence of this sonnet—the mysterious ability of a short, strict form to enclose broad emotional spaces—amplifies its subject. Enforcing the *volta*'s shift from general to particular, "love's function" in the octave to the sestet's "lovers," Cummings' poem composes metaphysical complexities of love and concretizes them, "Centring the eye on their essential human element."[16]

"SONG" (CP 776)

but we've the may
(for you are in love
and i am)to sing,
my darling:while
old worlds and young
(big little and all
worlds)merely have
the must to say

and the when to do
is exactly theirs
(dull worlds or keen;
big little and all)
but lose or win
(come heaven,come hell)
precisely ours
is the now to grow

it's love by whom
(my beautiful friend)
the gift to live
is without until:
but pitiful they've
(big little and all)
no power beyond
the trick to seem

their joys turn woes
and right goes wrong
(dim worlds or bright;
big little and all)

Love's Function

whereas(my sweet)
our summer in fall
and in winter our spring
is the yes of yes

love was and shall
be this only truth
(a dream of a deed,
born not to die)
but worlds are made
of hello and goodbye:
glad sorry or both
(big little and all)

Though Cummings might go amaying in October (see "notice the convulsed orange inch of moon," *CP* 86), the "may" of "SONG" is love's ideal season. In this month not only of flowers but permission, words spring from one grammatical function to another, and a two-beat line can dance rhythmically past "big little and all/ worlds" into a realm where "the gift to live/ is without until." Sprightliest of cavalier poems, "SONG" sings so joyfully the delights of surrender and dismisses so neatly the dead alternative that it transcends its own genre. Raising seduction to the level of philosophic proposition, though with never a didactic syllable, it builds an Archimedean lever, sets love on one end, and easily moves the world.

Motion is everything here, and stanza one exemplifies many of the ways this poem, traveling light, achieves it. The unusual, initial "but," for example, conveying the thrust of prior conversation, sets compactly the cavalier scene, while a lively pun on "may" links senses of right and spring; "we've the may/ . . . to sing," notes the amorous speaker, justifying his advances in love's name, and he simultaneously implies that if they do, a metaphoric spring, "May," will follow. Like Donne's persona in "The Sunne Rising"—"She'is all States, and all Princes, I,/ Nothing else is"[17]—Cummings' lover so-lipsistically acknowledges real existence only in the love of his lady and himself. Thus, "old worlds and young/ (big little and all/ worlds)" dwindle into insignificance next to the lovers. Recalling "may," a matching pun on "must" underscores this contrast. The decay of mold as well as the tug of obligation attaches to the "must to say," thematically and structurally counterbalancing the celebrative, musical "may/ . . . to sing."

Following stanzas enrich the pattern of movement and contrast. In two, the vague and abstract "when to do," specifying neither time nor action, emphasizes by juxtaposition the particular, kinetic "now to grow." Thriving on experience—"(come heaven,come hell)" is a Faustian imperative as well as a subjunctive balancing of possibility—lovers transcend it by growth; but "(dull worlds or keen;/ big little and all)" are limited to mere existence. In earlier poems, Cummings had often used "world" neutrally, alloting it significance primarily through modification or context—"let the world say 'his wisest music stole/ nothing from death'" (*CP* 306); "A world of made/ is not a world of born" (*CP* 554)—but his final, most firmly transcendent poems reject "world" entirely. It becomes a metaphysical shorthand, a concretization of empirically bounded existence, what one might call a de-personification: human beings committed to reason rather than feeling make a "world." Thus, lovers share "the gift to live/ . . . without until," a two-fold living present in a reality above time, but "pitiful" worlds have "no power beyond/ the trick to seem." Apparent shadow is an alternative poor indeed to emotional substance.

In wrongsideout "worlds," the inversion of substance and shadow deforms all values; "their joys turn woes/ and right goes wrong." Lovers, though, rise above the limitations of external reality and create a perpetual warmth by feeling; whatever the season, they have spring and summer. Transcendently substantial love is λόγος, "(a dream of a deed,/ born not to die)." Platonically shadowy "worlds," however, remain mired in the "malady of the quotidian";[18] to their linear comings and goings, "hello and goodbye," "time will not relent."

"all worlds have halfsight,seeing either with" (CP 845)

> all worlds have halfsight,seeing either with
>
> life's eye(which is if things seem spirits)or
> (if spirits in the guise of things appear)
> death's:any world must always half perceive.
>
> Only whose vision can create the whole
>
> (being forever born a foolishwise
> proudhumble citizen of ecstasies
> more steep than climb can time with all his years)
>
> he's free into the beauty of the truth;
>
> and strolls the axis of the universe
> —love. Each believing world denies,whereas
> your lover(looking through both life and death)
> timelessly celebrates the merciful
>
> wonder no world deny may or believe

Cummings' last poem on love, "all worlds have halfsight," closes, as it should, his collection. The fitting summation of a life's work of celebrative ecstasy, this splendid sonnet is nearly as final in tone and vision as Yeats's "Under Ben Bulben," as ascendant as the *Divina Commedia*'s last canto. Yet it is distinctly Cummings' own. Discoursing in a clear, lofty, and rhythmically remarkable voice, the poet sings once more of love's function and its power. Finding yet another image with which to concretize his metaphysic, he gives his subject a last and lasting liveliness.

Optically, one eye will serve, though two are better; in the metaphorical expansion of "all worlds have halfsight," one eye is blind, but two make up a visionary company. Cummings rejects here "all worlds," because, incurably monocular, they lack the integrating faculty of depth perception; "seeing either with/ life's eye" or with "death's," they fail to grasp the relation of all things on the continuum of human experience.

Worlds—they are again, as in "SONG" (*CP 776*), a concretization of bounded reason in contrast to the miraculous transcendence of lovers—are limited points of reference, incomplete syntheses. Their vision is flattened to either the diaphanous film of the ethereal, "(which is if things seem spirits)," or the opaque plane of the mundane, "(if spirits in the guise of things appear)." Unable to unite yet keep distinct the soul and the body, the transcendental *allgemeine* and the *besondere* through which we know it, "any world must always half perceive."

Lovers, however, know the full depth of being; "looking through both life and death"—Cummings neatly alters Tennyson's phrase to suggest binocular vision as well as transcendence[19]—they coordinate dextrous and sinister eyes to make a multidimensional vision of the whole. Unchecked by appearance—when "things *seem* spirits" or "spirits in the *guise* of things *appear*"—they look beyond it; undeterred by the apparent diversity of phenomena—when "*things* seem *spirits*" or "*spirits* in the guise of *things* appear"—they conceive essential unity. "Forever born," the lover is both immortal and yet constantly, by growth, created anew; "forever born a . . . citizen of ecstasies," he "can create" as well. Thus, though his ecstasies are "steep"—emotionally costly as well as literally taxing in the ascent—"he's free into the beauty of the truth."

Halfsighted worlds, like the two-dimensional men of flatland, misconstrue the nature of the universe around them; limited to the rational dimensions of time and space, they neither visualize the vastness beyond them nor even suspect that it exists. Worlds look *at* phenomena; "believing," they deny, for the two are sides of the same phenomenological coin: to believe in the vision of "life's eye" or of "death's" is to deny their miraculous unity, the oneness of flesh and spirit. Creative lovers traffic in no such coin; they look *through* phenomena. Conceiving existence to be a "merciful wonder," a miracle beyond the limiting scope of belief or denial, they timelessly celebrate it.

A triumph of "all worlds" is its rich specificity—Cummings' poetic craft breathes life into everything it touches here, even the stony abstractions of timelessness and transcendent unity—but it is the speaker's remarkable voice that most moves us. Cummings had written, "my father's voice was so magnificent that he was called on to impersonate God speaking from Beacon Hill";[20] this poem displays a vocal legacy. Lofty, slow, and serene, the vatic persona weighs grandly a plenitude of spondees—I scan eight in the sonnet's fourteen lines—and moves with absolute assurance through the vast latitudes of this poem's prosody. Now declaiming in immediate loose sentences —"all worlds have halfsight"; "Each believing world denies"— now delaying sense with the orator's flourish of periodicity— "the merciful/ wonder no world deny may or believe"—this striking voice shapes pace and tension into an utterance of final vision. Having climbed to it, Cummings ceased to write and went "free into the beauty of the truth."

7

CONCLUSION

When old age shall this generation waste,
Thou shalt remain, in midst of other woe
Than ours, a friend to man . . .

—John Keats,
"*Ode on a Grecian Urn*"

I

"Art," an old saw runs, "is a lie that makes us see the truth." The art of E. E. Cummings is both this and its opposite, a truth that makes us see the lie. Harnessing the lie of order, of technical and imaginative precision in a chaotic world, Cummings' poems ride it past wordly limitations to a transcendent truth. Their commitment to that truth, however, is so unqualified as to reject any compromise. And so the poems, when they are not extolling the "mystery-of-mysteries" who is "love,"[1] are vigilantly exposing the lives from which love is absent and the lies told to mask that absence.

We must avoid reacting comfortably to the word "love." By it, Cummings meant not only ἔρος and ἀγάπη but a dynamic coherence; love is the name not only for what she and he, amaying or octobering, practice, or the poet, pondering dooms of love, feels for his father, but also for the principle of cyclic change. It is the force that through the green fuse drives the flower and the force that blasts the roots of trees, the movement through death to growth that makes possible the movement from selfhood to self-transcendence. If none of this is unique, we may note that Cummings' vision is made special by its intensity. In affirmation, the poet achieves a rare and heightened joy, a plane on which exultation and serenity interpenetrate and swell each other. In negation, he proudly sustains the child's egocentric refusal to accept excuses. "You *promised*," shouts the child, and will not be comforted on a circusless Sunday; "you've *promise*," insists the poet, and will tolerate no reasonable explanation for the failure to realize it.

II

If all this sounds abstract or even petulant, we must remember, with Huxley, that "thought is coarse, material unimaginably subtle." Cummings was a poet, and his task as such was to transform, by the subtle alchemic of linguistic material, leaden thought into precious feeling. The magic-maker's wand —what is perhaps his greatest gift—is his facility for invention. Cummings waves it and a spring, mud-luscious and puddle-wonderful, appears before our eyes; another wave—"1 law for the lions &/ oxen is science)" (*CP* 791)—and William Blake is conjured up and speaking to our century.

No need, I think, to catalogue these effects. Even a cursory reading of Cummings will show that he heeded Ezra Pound's dictum, "Make it new," with a unique emphasis upon the verb. "Obsessed by Making" (*CP* 223), this poet never contented himself with the ordinary possibilities of syntax, typography, or diction; instead, he tried to rekindle the embers of burnt-out words by stirring them. Because he succeeded as well as he did, Cummings' best poems disconnect the safety device of cerebral response. Whether praising—"nobody,not even the rain,has such small hands" (*CP* 366)—or damning—"why must itself up every of a park/ anus stick some quote statue unquote" (*CP* 636)—they strike us with the impact of significant personal experience: "(now the ears of [our] ears awake and/ now the eyes of [our] eyes are opened)" (*CP* 663).

III

What the opening of our deepest eyes and ears finally achieves is the possibility of literal insight. The distinguished contemporary poet John Logan has put it well. Of "that melancholy" (*CP* 697), the poem in which an organ grinder's assistant, Mr bowing Cockatto, "proffers the meaning of the stars" on "one . . . piece/ of pitiful paper—", Logan explains:

> the long-laboring (grinding) musician of Cummings' poem is also a figure for the poet, and in presenting us with an oracular white cockatoo, the poet holds out to us himself. However, as the poem makes clear, the organ-grinder will not tap the creature's cage unless we ask him to. We seldom ask. I think it is because even if we understand this—that if we let him the poet gives

us himself—still we may not understand the truth behind: that what the poet offers us is not so much himself . . ., but by a self-transcendence, *our*selves.[2]

It is impossible to read Cummings sensitively without redis-
covering "the meaning of [our] stars" and of ourselves. If in
the satires this poet seems sometimes a twentieth-century Diogenes, looking for self-fulfilled human beings instead of honest
men, the lamp of his poetry is nonetheless real illumination for
those who will heed it. And if in his lyrics we sometimes meet
people who seem too common or too uncommon to be very
much like us, an openhearted embrace of them can lead us,
like the samaritan in "a man who had fallen among thieves"
(*CP* 258), to "a million billion trillion stars." Above all, a
twice generous reading of Cummings will teach us that in the
poet's gift of self—"man . . . fiend . . . angel . . . coward, clown,
traitor, idiot, dreamer, beast" (*CP* 562)—all selves are given,
each for his own receiving. As Emerson wrote, "He is most us."[3]

IV

The business of ranking poets is better left to disinterested
observers—best of all, perhaps, simply left—but an admirer,
like a clear-sighted lover, does well to assess strengths and
weaknesses. In Cummings the strengths are primary, as I hope
the preceding chapters have shown: a firm and affirmative vision, structural discipline, and the magical power to make language "stir and squirm" (*CP* 520). There are weaknesses as
well, of course, and for me they are of two kinds. First, the
intensity of Cummings' vision limited him in range, so that we
get too many poems of the same sort. Ingenuity and skill may
abate this failing, but the reader of all Cummings' poems is apt
to feel his work both thematically and technically repetitious.
More crucial, I think, is a certain lack of sinew, a vocal strain-
ing as in Blake that bespeaks the distance between artist and
audience. Yeats the visionary poet rubbed elbows with the

world, and the friction humanized him. Cummings, though no hermit, remained aloof.

Withal, he is one of the major poets of our century, original and gifted. Limited in ways some poets have not been, he had the compensation of unique and prepossessing talents, and his finest poems seem to me permanently interesting. Posterity, the nag of time, is always a dark horse; but I believe that as long as human beings seek truth and beauty, Cummings' poems will listen to them, and speak.

NOTES

CHAPTER 1
INTRODUCTION

1. See Cummings' *i: six nonlectures* (New York: Atheneum, 1962), p. 5.
2. Both quotations are from the *Journals*, in *Ralph Waldo Emerson: Selected Prose and Poetry*, ed. Reginald L. Cook (New York: Holt, Rinehart and Winston, 1950), pp. 476 and 475. The hobgoblin passage is from "Self Reliance": "A foolish consistency is the hobgoblin of little minds, adored by little statesmen and philosophers and divines. With consistency a great soul has simply nothing to do. . . . Speak what you think now in hard words and to-morrow speak what to-morrow thinks in hard words again, though it contradicts everything you said to-day" (*Selected Prose and Poetry*, p. 172).
3. Review of Cummings' *1x1, The Nation* (April 1, 1944), reprinted in Miss Moore's *Predilections* (New York: Viking, 1955), p. 140.
4. Stanton A. Coblentz, quoted by Alex Jackinson in *Congress Weekly*, XVIII (August 20, 1951), 13, and reprinted in *EΣTI: eec: E. E. Cummings and the Critics*, ed. S. V. Baum (East Lansing, Michigan: Michigan State University Press, 1962), p. 176.
5. Yvor Winters, ["Merely a Penumbra"], *American Literature*, X (January, 1939), 520. Reprinted in *E. E. Cummings and the Critics*, p. 98.
6. "A Poet's Own Way," *The New York Times Book Review* (October 31, 1954), 6. Reprinted in *E. E. Cummings and the Critics*, p. 192.
7. *i: six nonlectures*, pp. 5–6.
8. Wallace Stevens' cycle of desire, fulfillment, and ennui makes an interesting contrast to Cummings': while the intellectual poetry of Stevens drives always toward a sensory hedonism, Cummings' often sensuous poems aspire to ideal spirituality.
9. Letter to Paul Rosenfeld, quoted in *i: six nonlectures*, p. 9.

10. Hart Crane, "Legend," *The Complete Poems and Selected Letters and Prose of Hart Crane*, ed. Brom Weber (New York: Liveright, 1966), p. 3.
11. *i: six nonlectures*, p. 29.
12. Ibid.
13. Ibid.
14. Ibid.
15. W. B. Yeats, "The Second Coming," *The Collected Poems of W. B. Yeats* (New York: Macmillan, 1956), p. 185.
16. *Predilections*, p. 140.
17. The passages are from William Wordsworth, "My Heart Leaps Up," *Wordsworth's Poetical Works*, ed. E. de Selincourt (Oxford: Oxford University Press, 1940–1949), 5 vols., I, 226.
18. Barry Marks, in his generally persuasive *E. E. Cummings* (New Haven: Twayne, 1964), argues in favor of this poem. He notes "the fullness with which Cummings entered into the mind and heart and even the speech patterns of the child-speaker" and distinguishes "an important quality of irony [that] qualifies the value of the child's love" (p. 53). I can only express my disagreement. As a fellow lover of Cummings, I share Mr. Marks's desire to explain away this poem; I think, however, his analysis here is too ingenious.
19. Quoted in Charles Norman, *E. E. Cummings: The Magic-Maker* (New York: Duell, Sloan and Pearce, 1964), rev. ed., p. 214.

CHAPTER 2
A PLEASANT COUNTRY

1. Love is of course not to be equated with the sexual act *per se*— Cummings' keen satire cuts through the professional veneer of a dead-to-life prostitute in "raise the shade" (*CP* 109)—but even a casual embrace has often lively and positive emotional consequences. See, for example, "may i feel said he" (*CP* 399).
2. "Peter Quince at the Clavier," *The Palm at the End of the Mind: Selected Poems and a Play by Wallace Stevens*, ed. Holly Stevens (New York: Alfred A. Knopf, 1971), p. 10.
3. Robert Browning, "My Last Duchess," *Browning: Poetical Works* (Oxford: Oxford University Press, 1940), p. 318.
4. Cummings follows here the example of his friend Ezra Pound's early work.
5. *Delia*, Sonnet XLVI, in *Renaissance England*, ed. Roy Lamson and Hallett Smith (New York: W. W. Norton, 1942), p. 648.

6. See, for example, Sonnet XVIII of those in Laura's lifetime, "Vergognando talor ch'ancor se taccia."
7. William Empson in *The Strand*, quoted by William York Tindall, *A Reader's Guide to Dylan Thomas* (New York: Farrar, Straus & Giroux, 1962), p. 181.
8. Sonnets III and VII of *Astrophel and Stella*, in *Renaissance England*, pp. 237 and 239.
9. Sonnet CXXIV in Laura's lifetime. The translation is Wollaston's.
10. Section I of "Spring and All," *The Collected Earlier Poems of William Carlos Williams* (New York: New Directions, 1951), pp. 241–242.
11. "Sailing to Byzantium," *The Collected Poems of W. B. Yeats*, p. 191. The following quotation is from the same poem.

CHAPTER 3
SO MANY SELVES

1. "Birches," *Selected Poems of Robert Frost* (New York: Holt, Rinehart and Winston, 1963), p. 78.
2. See "After Apple-Picking," *Selected Poems of Robert Frost*, pp. 52–53.
3. This tradition is the slight but happy offspring of a heavy and infelicitous parent, Francis Quarles' *Emblems, Divine and Moral* (1635). Now as then, moral injunction and a distinguishable piety characterize the form. Here the words of little you-i are an analog to the scriptural citation that accompanied an emblem; they are the caption to Cummings' implied picture.
4. "The Love Song of J. Alfred Prufrock," *T. S. Eliot: Collected Poems 1909–1962* (New York: Harcourt, Brace and World, 1963), p. 3. Further quotations are from the same poem.
5. The earlier *Poems: 1923–1954* reads: "your f.ing flag"; only censorship, however, prevented Cummings from having "the honest word 'fuck' printed As Is" (*L* 234)—his instruction to the German translators of *The Enormous Room*, Elisabeth and Helmuth Braem. An earlier outrage at editorial nicety occurs in a letter to Pound (*L* 136): "as 1 castration complex to another:'fuck' has been changed to 'trick' in new [*New English Weekly*] today arriving with editor's compliments. This(said our hero with illdisguised restraint)settles the ? of Angleterre."
6. From a letter to Paul Rosenfeld, quoted in Cummings' *i: six nonlectures*, p. 8.

7. "Mr. Housman's Message," *Personae: The Collected [Shorter] Poems of Ezra Pound* (New York: New Directions, 1926), p. 44.
8. "The Laws of God, the Laws of Man," *The Collected Poems of A. E. Housman* (New York: Holt, Rinehart and Winston, 1965), p. 111. A comparison of the two poets, though simplifying drastically, seems to isolate their transatlantic difference. Both Housman and Cummings wanted freedom from the religious and moral strictures of their times—the English poet asked, "let God and man decree/ Laws for themselves and not for me" (*AEH* 111)—but only the American could find the independence to realize that freedom. Housman, captive of God, fate, or Victorian decorum, was forced from without:

> And since, my soul, we cannot fly
> To Saturn nor to Mercury,
> Keep we must, if keep we can,
> The foreign laws of God and man. (*AEH* 111)

Cummings cheerfully resisted external power, "the pomp of must and shall" (*CP* 520); "for any ruffian of the sky," his hero "doesn't give a damn" (*CP* 774). Cummings plays elsewhere with Housman's poems. His morally pointed recasting of the Ares-Aphrodite story (*CP* 799) resembles Terence Hearsay's appeal to the legend of Mithridates. Echoing Housman's laconic conclusion—"I tell the tale that I heard told./ Mithridates, he died old." (*AEH* 90)—Cummings' poem ends: "my tragic tale concludes herewith:/ soldier,beware of mrs smith."
9. "The Idea of Order at Key West," *The Palm at the End of the Mind*, p. 98.
10. Wallace Stevens, "Sunday Morning," *The Palm at the End of the Mind*, p. 7.
11. "Sunday Morning," *The Palm at the End of the Mind*, p. 8.
12. W. B. Yeats, "The Gyres," *The Collected Poems of W. B. Yeats*, p. 291. As responses to a world gone mad, this poem and Cummings'—both were written in the late 1930s—have much in common. Indeed, the parallels extend through subject to language:

> What matter though numb nightmare ride on top,
> And blood and mire the sensitive body stain? (*WBY*)

> then let men kill which cannot share
> let blood and flesh be mud and mire. (*EEC*)

13. W. B. Yeats, "Lapis Lazuli," *The Collected Poems of W. B. Yeats*, p. 292.

14. A letter of Cummings' (*L* 270–271) substantiates my reading in most respects. Here, however, Cummings' paraphrase makes "earth" the implied referrent of "her." Since "grass is flesh," the difference is not one of spirit.
15. W. B. Yeats, "Byzantium," *The Collected Poems of W. B. Yeats*, p. 243.
16. W. B. Yeats, "The Circus Animals' Desertion," *The Collected Poems of W. B. Yeats*, p. 336.
17. *An Essay On Man*, II, 3–4 and 8. The adage near the close of this paragraph is also Pope's phrasing, II, 1, from the same poem.
18. In a letter to an unidentified English correspondent (*L* 244), Cummings asks: "concerning the 'small "I"':did it never strike you as significant that,of all God's children,only English & Americans apotheosize their egos by capitalizing a pronoun whose equivalent is in French 'je',in German 'ich',& in Italian 'io'?"

CHAPTER 4
DYING IS FINE

1. "A slumber did my spirit seal," *Wordsworth's Poetical Works*, II, 216.
2. "And Death Shall Have No Dominion," *The Collected Poems of Dylan Thomas* (New York: New Directions, 1957), p. 77.
3. The fabulous texture of Cummings' poem may owe something to Paul Claudel's "Le sombre mai," though there is not in the French poem the elaborate patterned development of "All in green." See Claudel's *Poésies* (Paris: Gallimard, 1970), p. 15.
4. "Easter 1916," *The Collected Poems of W. B. Yeats*, p. 179.
5. W. B. Yeats, "Death," *The Collected Poems of W. B. Yeats*, p. 230.
6. "Sunday Morning," *The Palm at the End of the Mind*, p. 7.
7. A feminine attribution, though from a less interesting poem, occurs in "if i should sleep with a lady called death" (*CP* 161).
8. "Peter Quince at the Clavier," *The Palm at the End of the Mind*, p. 10.
9. "The tragedy of sexual intercourse," remarked Yeats, who in many ways found it not tragic, "is the perpetual virginity of the souls" (quoted in A. N. Jeffares, *A Commentary on the Collected Poems of W. B. Yeats* [Stanford, California: Stanford University Press, 1968], p. 372). Cummings in "suppose" uses sexual allegory to ameliorate that tragedy; the prospective union of Death and After-

wards ends a spiritual virginity, exposing souls to the transcendent possibilities of growth.

10. W. B. Yeats, "Death," *The Collected Poems of W. B. Yeats*, p. 230.

11. Cummings recorded this poem and others, together with passages from *Him, Eimi*, and *Santa Claus*, for Caedmon records (TC 1017). The interested listener will want to hear the same wonderfully modulated voice reading *i: six nonlectures*, Caedmon TC 1186–1191. Here, amidst observations and narrative, Cummings reads several of his poems not on the single album.

12. Sylvia Plath would later explore this image, its tone wholly altered, in her poem "Edge":

> The woman is perfected.
> Her dead
>
> Body wears the smile of accomplishment,
> The illusion of a Greek necessity
>
> Flows in the scrolls of her toga . . .

Ariel (New York: Harper and Row, 1966), p. 84.

13. "The Figure a Poem Makes," *Selected Prose of Robert Frost*, ed. Cox and Lathem (New York: Holt, Rinehart and Winston, 1966), p. 18.

14. "The Poet," *Ralph Waldo Emerson: Selected Prose and Poetry*, p. 319.

15. Ibid.

16. "Ode on a Grecian Urn," *Keats' Poetical Works*, ed. H. W. Garrod (Oxford: Oxford University Press, 1958), p. 261.

CHAPTER 5
FURNISHED SOULS

1. *The Complete Poems of Emily Dickinson*, ed. Thomas H. Johnson (Boston: Little, Brown, 1960), p. 191.

2. Ibid.

3. Burton Rascoe describes a wonderful Cummings monologue in Paris in the twenties: "At one point he convulsed us with a recital of a whole episode from 'Hiawatha,' with a sententiousness which made the banality of that banal poem insupportable." Quoted in Charles Norman's *E. E. Cummings: The Magic-Maker*, p. 149.

4. For the common romantic association of moon and imagination, one might see Cummings' early poem, "who knows if the moon's" (*CP*

129) or the later "who is this" (*CP* 831). Notably, both are interrogative, reinforcing the poet's claim that "more than know means guess" (*CP* 390). Doubtless, Cummings' moon owes something to Yeats, who concerned himself with both lunar imagination and interrogative vision.

5. Cummings' letter to Paul Rosenfeld, quoted in the poet's *i: six nonlectures*, p. 8.

6. The poems referred to are: "i sing of Olaf glad and big" (*CP* 339); "little joe gould has lost his teeth and doesn't know where" (*CP* 410); "my father moved through dooms of love" (*CP* 520); "if there are any heavens my mother will(all by herself)have" (*CP* 352); "in heavenly realms of hellas dwelt" (*CP* 799); and "anyone lived in a pretty how town" (*CP* 515).

7. The particular monologue in question continued for "Eight solid hours . . . and never a repetition." Burton Rascoe, quoted in *E. E. Cummings: The Magic-Maker*, pp. 149–150.

8. Speaking ill, of course, is quite different from speaking a dialect. To speak ill is to reveal by one's choice of words a furnished soul, whereas to speak a dialect may reveal nothing more than a physical origin. The distinction is worth making because those who attack Cummings as anti-Semitic often confuse it. Dialogue may damn in Cummings' poems, as in "ygUDuh" (*CP* 547), but it may praise too; "i say no world" (*CP* 523), with its vast love for "one/ unsellable not buyable alive/ one i say human being)one/ goldberger," effectively demonstrates this.

9. The quotations are from "The Hollow Men," *T. S. Eliot: Collected Poems 1909–1962*, pp. 81–82. For the reference to Swift, see Pt. III of *Gulliver's Travels*.

10. "How I Do Not Love Italy," *Vanity Fair* (October, 1926). Reprinted in *E. E. Cummings: A Miscellany Revised*, ed. George J. Firmage (New York: October House, 1965), p. 168.

11. "Memorabilia," *Browning: Poetical Works*, p. 245.

12. *Der Tod in Venedig* (Frankfurt am Main: Fischer, 1954), p. 17. H. T. Lowe-Porter translates thus: "When one wanted to arrive overnight at the incomparable, the fabulous, the like-nothing-else-in-the-world, where was it one went? Why, obviously . . . ."

13. The letter quoted is after a later trip, in 1956, but the poet's earlier feelings about Venice had undergone no drastic change.

14. *Browning: Poetical Works*, p. 226.

15. See "The force that through the green fuse drives the flower," *The Collected Poems of Dylan Thomas*, p. 10, and Canto 33 of the

Paradiso. Thomas' poem was written some eight years after Cummings'.

16. *The Complete Poems of Emily Dickinson,* p. 327.
17. *Him* (New York: Liveright, 1970), p. 11.
18. "There was a saviour," *The Collected Poems of Dylan Thomas,* p. 140.
19. "The Lay of Ike," *The Dream Songs* (New York: Farrar, Straus & Giroux, 1969), p. 25.
20. Yeats regarded his poems "The Cap and Bells" and "He Wishes for the Cloths of Heaven" as, respectively, the right and wrong ways to try to win a lady, and Richard Ellmann has contrasted Wallace Stevens' "The Emperor of Ice-Cream" and "Cortège for Rosenbloom" as the right and wrong ways to conduct a funeral. "Little Effie" belongs to a similar pairing: the active love of "a man who had fallen among thieves" (*CP* 258) is the right way to be a Christian, the fearful obedience of "little Effie" the wrong.
21. See *Principles of Morals and Legislation* (1789).
22. *The Poetry and Prose of William Blake,* ed. David Erdman (Garden City, New York: Doubleday, 1965), p. 43.

CHAPTER 6
LOVE'S FUNCTION

1. *Agamemnon,* first chorus, ll. 250–251.
2. "Death be not proud" (Holy Sonnet X), *Donne's Poetical Works,* ed. H. J. C. Grierson (Oxford: Oxford University Press, 1912), 2 vols., I, 326.
3. *The Collected Poems of Dylan Thomas,* p. 77.
4. *Wordsworth's Poetical Works,* IV, 57.
5. See William Faulkner, *The Bear,* Ch. 1.
6. "Directive," *Selected Poems of Robert Frost,* p. 252.
7. James Dickey, "The Leap," *Poems 1957–1967* (Middletown, Connecticut: Wesleyan University Press, 1967), p. 285.
8. Not surprisingly, this poem has been set to music—twice, in fact. Josef Alexander composed music for a chorus of mixed voices, four part, *a capella* (New York: Lawson-Gould Music Publishers, 1956), and Charles Hamm made a musical setting for voice and piano (Northhampton, Massachusetts: Valley Music Press, 1956).
9. A letter from Cummings to Norman Friedman, quoted in Friedman's *E. E. Cummings: The Art of His Poetry* (Baltimore: Johns Hopkins University Press, 1960), p. 65.

10. Marianne Moore, "Marriage," *The Complete Poems of Marianne Moore* (New York: Viking/Macmillan, 1967), p. 62.
11. *Paradiso* 33.61–4. The translation is Louis Biancolli's (New York: Washington Square Press, 1966), 3 vols., III, 134. Perhaps Villon's "Ballade des Dames du Temps Jadis" will also help here: "Mais òu sont les neiges d'antan?"
12. "The Waking," *The Collected Poems of Theodore Roethke* (Garden City, New York: Doubleday, 1965), p. 108.
13. *Adventures in Value: Fifty Photographs by Marion Morehouse, Text by E. E. Cummings* (New York: Harcourt, Brace and World, 1962), III, 1, n. p.
14. "Meditations of an Old Woman": "First Meditation," *The Collected Poems of Theodore Roethke*, p. 157.
15. Having seen the beatific vision, Dante closes his poem thus:

> All' alta fantasia qui mancò possa;
> Ma già volgeva il mio disiro e il *velle*,
> Sì come rota ch' egualmenta è mossa,
> L' amor che move il sole e l' altre stelle.

> The strength for this high fantasy was gone now.
> But at last my will and my desire—
> Like a wheel moving evenly—were revolving
> From the love that moves the sun and all the stars.
> (Biancolli's translation)

In "Burnt Norton," Eliot speaks of "the still point of the turning world": "there the dance is,/ But neither arrest nor movement." *T. S. Eliot: Collected Poems 1909–1962*, p. 177.
16. W. H. Auden, "The Model," *Collected Shorter Poems 1927–1957* (New York: Random House, 1967), p. 216.
17. *Donne's Poetical Works*, I, 11.
18. Wallace Stevens, "The Man Whose Pharynx Was Bad," *The Palm at the End of the Mind*, p. 52. The phrase that ends this paragraph is from the same poem.
19. Tennyson had written of the poet: "He saw through life and death, through good and ill,/ He saw through his own soul." "The Poet," *The Poems of Tennyson*, ed. Christopher Ricks (London: Longmans, 1969), p. 222. But the Laureate's thrice-dowered poet—"the hate of hate, the scorn of scorn,/ The love of love"—is clearly not Cummings, who, embracing the third portion, rejects at least the second out of hand.

20. A letter to Paul Rosenfeld, quoted in Cummings' *i: six nonlectures*, pp. 8–9.

CHAPTER 7
CONCLUSION

1. Cummings' *i: six nonlectures*, p. 11.
2. "The Organ-Grinder and the Cockatoo: An Introduction to E. E. Cummings," in *Modern American Poetry: Essays in Criticism*, ed. Jerome Mazzaro (New York: David McKay, 1970), pp. 250–251. Mr. Logan's essay seems to me particularly fine in its poet's sense of the value of poetry and the value of Cummings.
3. "The Poet," *Ralph Waldo Emerson: Selected Prose and Poetry*, p. 3.

BIBLIOGRAPHIC NOTE

Among Cummings' works, most crucial for the poetry are *Complete Poems 1913–1962* (New York: Harcourt Brace Jovanovich, 1972) and *i: six nonlectures* (New York: Atheneum, 1962). Useful, too—and vastly entertaining—are the *Selected Letters of E. E. Cummings* (ed. F. W. Dupee and George Stade; New York: Harcourt, Brace and World, 1969) and *E. E. Cummings: A Miscellany Revised* (ed. George J. Firmage; New York: October House, 1965). Other important works are *The Enormous Room* (New York: Random House, 1934) and *Him* (New York: Liveright, 1955). A full listing of primary materials is given by the poet's bibliographer, George J. Firmage: *E. E. Cummings: A Bibliography* (Middletown, Connecticut: Wesleyan University Press, 1960).

Among the chief critical studies of Cummings are Norman Friedman's *e. e. cummings: the art of his poetry* (Baltimore: Johns Hopkins University Press, 1960), Barry Marks's *E. E. Cummings* (New Haven: Twayne, 1964), and Robert Wegner's *The Poetry and Prose of E. E. Cummings* (New York: Harcourt, Brace and World, 1965). Important collections of criticism are edited by S. V. Baum (ΕΣΤΙ: *eec: E. E. Cummings and the Critics*; East Lansing, Michigan: Michigan State University Press, 1962) and Norman Friedman (*E. E. Cummings: A Collection of Critical Essays*; Englewood Cliffs, New Jersey: Prentice-Hall, 1972). A new biography is now in progress, but though it may replace some factual gaps in Charles Norman's *E. E. Cummings: The Magic-Maker* (New York: Duell, Sloan and Pearce, rev. ed., 1964), it is unlikely to surpass that touching volume in immediacy. Extensive bibliographies of Cummings criticism are provided in Friedman's *E. E. Cummings: The Art of His Poetry* and Baum's *E. E. Cummings and the Critics*.

GENERAL INDEX

The page numbers set in italic indicate that the poem has been discussed extensively on those pages.

Aeschylus, *Agamemnon*, 94
Alexander, Josef, 124
Archimedes, 106
Aristotle, 7
Arnold, Matthew, 30
Auden, W. H., 41, 87; "The Unknown Citizen," 41; "The Model," 105

Beowulf, 103
Bentham, Jeremy, 91; *Principles of Morals and Legislation*, 124
Berryman, John, *The Dream Songs*, 73, 88
Blake, William, 90, 113, 114; *The Marriage of Heaven and Hell*, 19, 91, 113
Braem, Elizabeth, 119
Braem, Helmuth, 119
Browning, Robert, 83; "My Last Duchess," 23; "Memorabilia," 83; "Home-Thoughts, from Abroad," 85

Carlyle, Thomas, 91
Chanson de Roland, 40
Chaucer, Geoffrey, 30
Claudel, Paul, "Le sombre mai," 121
Coblentz, Stanton, 5
Crane, Hart, 26; "Legend," 7
Cummings, E. E.
    "a kike is the most dangerous," 15–16
    "a man who had fallen among thieves," 114, 124
    "a politician is an arse upon," 90
    "a salesman is an it that stinks Excuse," 49, 75
    Adventures in Value, 103
    "All in green went my love riding," 5, *59–63*
    "all worlds have halfsight,seeing either with," 66, *108–110*

"now air is air and thing is thing:no bliss," 71
"o by the by," 27, *36–38*, 52
"O sweet spontaneous," 36, 66
"one's not half two. It's two are halves of one:," 37, *94–97*
"pity this busy monster,manunkind," 107
"POEM, OR BEAUTY HURTS MR. VINAL," 90
Poems: 1923–1954, 119
"proud of his scientific attitude," *77–81*
"PUELLA MEA," 23, 24–25
"raise the shade," 8, 118
"red-rag and pink-flag," *9–10*, 68
"r-p-o-p-h-e-s-s-a-g-r," 14–15
Santa Claus, 122
Selected Letters, 2, 27, 37, 44, 62, 69, 80, 83–84, 91, 119, 120
"she being Brand," 30
"so many selves(so many fiends and gods," *51–53*
"somewhere i have never travelled,gladly beyond," 113
"SONG," *105–107*, 108
"sonnet entitled how to run the world)," ix, 5, *48–51*, 123
"suppose," *63–67*
"'sweet spring is your," 71
"that famous fatheads find that each," 75
"that melancholy," 113–114
"the boys i mean are not refined," ix
"the Cambridge ladies who live in furnished souls," *74–77*
"to start,to hesitate;to stop," 71
"we)under)over,the thing of floating Of," 10
"what does little Ernest croon," 90
"when god decided to invent," *13*
"when god lets my body be," *56–59*
"who is this," 123
"who knows if the moon's," 27–28, 37, 68, 122–123
"why must itself up every of a park," 113
"wild(at our first)beasts uttered human words," *70–72*
"yes is a pleasant country:," ix, 26, *32–34*
"ygUDuh," 123
Cummings, Rev. Edward, 44, 78, 98, 110

Daniel, Samuel, *Delia*, 23
Dante, 78, 83, 87, 95, 104; *Inferno*, 79, 84; *Paradiso*, 87, 101–102, 104, 108, 125
Dickey, James, 87; "The Leap," 99

Dickinson, Emily, 75; "What Soft—Cherubic Creatures—," 75; "I dwell in Possibility—," 88

Diogenes, 114

Donne, John, 95; "Death be not proud," 96; "The Sunne Rising," 106

Dostoyevski, Fyodor, *Notes from Underground*, 103

Eliot, T. S., 87; *The Waste Land*, 31; "The Love Song of J. Alfred Prufrock," 37–38; "The Hollow Men," 81; "Burnt Norton," 104, 125

Ellmann, Richard, 124

Emerson, Ralph Waldo, 71; *Journals*, 3, 4; "Self Reliance," 4, 117; "The Poet," 72, 114

Empson, William, 24

Faulkner, William, *The Bear*, 97

Firmage, George J., ix

Forster, E. M., *Howards End*, 84

Freud, Sigmund, 43

Friedman, Norman, ix, 124

Frost, Robert, 87; "Birches," 36; "After Apple-Picking," 37; "The Figure a Poem Makes," 71; "Directive," 97

Goethe, Johann Wolfgang von, 71; *Faust*, 107

Hamm, Charles, 124

Herbert, George, "The Pulley," 37; "The Collar," 37

Hesse, Eva, 91

Homer, *Iliad*, 40

Hopkins, Gerard Manley, "Spring and Fall," 11

Horace, *Odes*, 12–13

Housman, A. E., 44, 120; "To an Athlete Dying Young," 44; "The laws of God, the laws of man," 44, 120; "Terence, this is stupid stuff:," 120

Howe, Julia Ward, 83; "Battle Hymn of the Republic," 84

Huxley, Aldous, 112

Jarrell, Randall, 6

Keats, John, 72; "Ode on a Grecian Urn," 72, 111

Lewis, Ted, 90

Logan, John, 113–114

Longfellow, Henry Wadsworth, 76; "Hiawatha," 122

Lowell, Robert, 87

Mann, Thomas, *Der Tod in Venedig*, 83

Marks, Barry, ix, 118

Index

133

Wordsworth, William, "My Heart Leaps Up," 14; "Anecdote for Fathers," 14; "A slumber did my spirit seal," 56; "The Tables Turned," 96

Yeats, William Butler, 47, 62, 71, 72, 82, 87, 114–115, 121, 123; "The Folly of Being Comforted," 23; "Sailing to Byzantium," 33; "The Gyres," 47, 120; "Lapis Lazuli," 47; "Leda and the Swan," 48; "Byzantium," 52; "The Circus Animals' Desertion," 52; "Easter 1916," 63; "Death," 64, 69; "Under Ben Bulben," 72, 108; "Discoveries," 73; "The Cap and Bells," 124; "He Wishes for the Cloths of Heaven," 124